Eduard König, Alexander James Campbell

The religious history of Israel

A discussion of the chief problems in Old Testament history as opposed to the

development theorists

Eduard König, Alexander James Campbell

The religious history of Israel
A discussion of the chief problems in Old Testament history as opposed to the development theorists

ISBN/EAN: 9783337104047

Printed in Europe, USA, Canada, Australia, Japan

Cover: Foto ©Lupo / pixelio.de

More available books at **www.hansebooks.com**

THE
RELIGIOUS HISTORY OF ISRAEL.

*A DISCUSSION OF THE CHIEF PROBLEMS IN OLD
TESTAMENT HISTORY AS OPPOSED TO
THE DEVELOPMENT THEORISTS.*

BY

DR. FRIEDRICH EDUARD KÖNIG,
THE UNIVERSITY, LEIPZIG.

Translated by

REV. ALEX. J. CAMPBELL, M.A.,
BARRY.

EDINBURGH:
T. & T. CLARK, 38 GEORGE STREET.
1885.

AUTHOR'S PREFACE.

———o———

WITHIN the last ten years the progress of a comparative science of religion has raised not a few fresh questions in the minds of those specially interested in an accurate understanding of the Old Testament theory of the Universe. In the course of my present work I have noticed how far the German writers on the Old Testament have succeeded during the past year in proving the assertions made by a comparative science of religion. As this proof lay along the line of investigation which I had marked out for myself, I have accordingly followed out its consequences in this present work.

My general aim, apart from mere criticism, is to bring out the facts of religious history, and to trace the connection which they necessarily have with their presupposed causes. This, accomplished in an impartial manner, is the aim of every pure historical science.

This aim I have endeavoured to carry out, not only by a full and satisfactory examination of the sources, but by a careful survey of scientific opinions — favourable and adverse. Thus unbiassed in my search for truth, I have endeavoured to provide a good position for the survey of Israel's ancient religious history, tracing the discussions connected with it up to its present position.

As the stability of the general argument is not weakened by the absence of references to the Hebrew, I am glad that I am able on this account to make this small work accessible to the general public—to the wide circle of minds at present interested in questions of religious history.

CONTENTS.

INTRODUCTION.

The Principles on which this Inquiry should be conducted—The Writings of Opponents—Hypotheses—The general Plan of the present Work, ... 1

CHAPTER I.

The Religion of the Majority of Israel at Moses' Time, . 11

CHAPTER II.

Negative Proof of an appointed Religion in Israel, . 21

CHAPTER III.

Positive Proof of an appointed Religion in Israel, . 27

CHAPTER IV.

Collection of Formal, and the Transition to the Definite, or Material, Inquiries, ... 41

CHAPTER V.

Did Jahvism first come into Existence since David?—Whence the Name Jahveh?—Did Jahvism originate Outside of Canaan?—Is the God of Israel a Form of Baal? . . 45

CHAPTER VI.

The Monotheism of Ancient Israel—The Ethical Monotheism of the Prophets, ... 69

CHAPTER VII.

The Being of Jahveh—Was Jahveh originally regarded as Fire?
—Jahveh Ssebaoth—Was Jahveh originally regarded as
Heaven?—Was Jahveh regarded by the Prophets merely as
an Idea? 85

CHAPTER VIII.

The Representation of Jahveh—The Image of the Bull—The
Ephod—The Symbolism of the Temple—The Images of
Baal and Astarte, ... 97

CHAPTER IX.

The Character of Jahveh—Human Sacrifices—Circumcision—
The Idea of Holiness, ... 129

CHAPTER X.

Jahveh's Covenant with Israel—The Covenant and the Priests—
The Priests and the Divine Guidance (Torah), . . 148

CHAPTER XI.

Jahvism viewed in the light of its Legal Beginnings—The
Position of the Acting and Writing Prophets with the view
to a correct Estimate of Morality, ... 163

CHAPTER XII.

Pre-prophetic Jahvism and the Universality of Prophecy—The
Religion of Ancient Israel individualistic—Israel's more
definite Universality—Israel a Nation and a Religious
Community, ... 172

CHAPTER XIII.

The Formal Dignity of the Religion of Pre-prophetic Israel—
Was the Religion of Ancient Israel of Natural Growth?—
Knowledge of the Effects derived from the Operation of the
Causes, ... 184

CONCLUSION, . . . 191

INTRODUCTION.

1. *The Motives which have induced us to follow out these Studies.* — Efforts like the present, made to throw light on the development of Old Testament history, need, in our day, no special apology. We undertake the present work, however, with greater interest, from the fact that Kuenen's ideas on the formation of Israel's Faith have recently been presented to the German mind in fresh surroundings. The appearance of such a book—inspired as it is with Kuenen's spirit—necessarily leads to a careful scrutiny of its parts, and a thorough investigation of its position as a whole. In following out such a course we give the work its due place in our theological literature, emanating as it does from the pen of one who is the modern representative of that school, whose aim, we are informed, is to present the purely scientific view of the origin and development of

the religion we meet with in Bible history. Looking at the past, we see that its theories, held even by such men as Kaiser,[1] Gramberg,[2] von Bohlen,[3] George,[4] and Vatke,[5] are now practically ignored, notwithstanding the efforts made by Daumer,[6] Ghillany,[7] Noack,[8] Scherr,[9] and von der Alm[10] to revive their memories and reconstruct their forms. Kuenen,[11] on the other hand, following in the footsteps of Dozy,[12] Oort,[13] Land,[14] and the other compeers of that school, has in several of his writings wrought out what we may regard as the modern idea of Israel's development. In this light Tiele[15] mentions him as his great predecessor, and seems to regard in his teaching a correct representation of Israel's historical nature and religious surroundings. In the list of Kuenen's followers we find such names as Duhm,[16] Wellhausen,[17] Smend,[18] Maybaum,[19] and Stade,[20] who speaks of his master's chief work "as the standard one on the development of Eastern religion." To such a list we might add the names of Goldziher[21] and Popper,[22] in their treatment of Old Testament mythology; as well as those of Pfleiderer[23] and von Hartmann,[24] in their views on the philosophy of religion.

An examination and comparison of these works referred to at the close of this Introduction we deem to be necessary for two reasons at least. In the first place, they contain, in a complete and what we might call representative form, a fair embodiment of views opposed to our own. And, secondly, we must remember that the views there enunciated are not altogether a thing of the past. They can with ease be reproduced, and, in the light of fresh surroundings, be presented anew as "entirely free from prejudice."

As our aim has been to bring before our readers those views for the most part common to our opponents, we have not quoted from all the works lying to our hand, but have referred only to those among the most recent which may be regarded as representative. Where, however, we have had to consider the opinions, or sift the views, of learned writers, we have been obliged more fully to notify their works and the passages referred to.

2. *The Hypotheses underlying our Investigations.*—Kuenen,[25] when dealing with the faiths of the Bible, proceeds on the following formulated bases. He says (in the special chapter, entitled "Unser Standpunct"): "Of these faiths Judaism is to us neither of less nor greater importance." "Judaism and Christianity certainly belong to the category of the greatest religious systems, but there is in reality between them and

all other systems no specific difference." "Judaism and Christianity, according to the belief of their respective followers, must no doubt radically differ from other faiths. But, in asserting that these systems have their origin in divine revelation, we must remember that the followers of Zarathustra, Sakja-Muni, and Mohammed hold the same belief as to the beginning of their respective systems." "Modern religious science does not now, as formerly, take its standpoint in the belief which admits no truth external to its own domains. It occupies a much wider basis,—that of impartial inquiry,—and is therefore able to notify and accept truth in all its forms, marking at the same time the varied phases which it, at intervals, assumes."

We, however, start from a somewhat different basis, in that we give no judgment as to the equality or difference of religious systems. We shall rather seek to regulate our ideas on the respective merits of the varied systems by a careful consideration of historical data. In this work we must not forget to examine the authority peculiar to the founders, and to look into the beliefs of the first disciples, associated as both are with their varied systems of religious thought.[26] To do so is indeed necessary for the full understanding and ample appreciation of all questions concerned with the origin and development of religious beliefs. Were we to do otherwise; were we, for example, to look to a system itself for the answer as to its origin, we would at best possess a superficial understanding of its nature, while, our course of inquiry would, *per se*, reveal a looseness of method and lack of judgment in its execution. It is in this respect that Kuenen seems to commit one of his fundamental errors, regarding, as he does, the belief possessed by the respective followers of Judaism and Christianity as something entirely apart from the conviction of the historical nature of their systems. In doing so he evidently intends to contrast these convictions, which are the offspring of knowledge, with the "unbiassed" estimate in which they are alike held by their respective opponents.

Kuenen's position [27] is also unsound when he describes modern religious science [28] as "the natural consequence of extended knowledge, and the further development of European genius throughout the past century." We differ from him in the idea of progress. We deem it as something substantial, and not merely visionary, something entirely free from misconceiving the true idea of the theory of the universe, or wrongly estimating the respective claims of Judaism and

Christianity. Progress, if it be genuine, should not lead to a denial of spirit, the hidden springs of the universe, all final causes, human freedom, the customary projects of mankind, the thought of sin, man's need and God-satisfying righteousness; in a word, to setting aside the truth contained in chapters i. 16-iii. 28 of Paul's Epistle to the Romans. This passage (thus rejected) seems to us to afford a strong foundation to all religious science. And we question the statement about his misconceptions of the prophetical and apostolical views of the universe being the necessary consequences of the development of true science. They have rather opened up to us a newer historical understanding of Judaism and Christianity, concerned as the leaders in modern religious thought have been, not so much with the comparisons of the varied systems, but with what we might term their adjustment. Their treatment of religious science, viewed in this light, will be seen to operate as a levelling process, freed altogether from comparative aims.

In their explanation of the Biblical narrative, the Development Theorists differ entirely from the views expressed by the sacred authors. Regarding this, we deem it of importance at the outset to confess, that as to the great principles of morality and faith our position is one of unison and harmony with that laid down in the divine Word. And it is evident, at least to our minds, "which of all these general theories, so long divided, will be the first to accept the simple facts of religious history." [29] Will it be the theory which many modern scientists base on the principle of evolution, or will it be that, which regards the prophets and apostles as the setters forth of Old Testament faith and morality? [30]

3. *The General Order of our Investigations.*—In this inquiry we must set before us a fair criticism of all views, and not the representation merely of the few, propounded, for example, by Vatke and Kuenen. We hope, however, to accomplish more than this, in establishing a way of our own, which we trust will approve itself to our readers as natural and simple, embracing at the same time all matters available in such a discussion.

---

1. Die Biblische Theologie, oder Judaismus und Christianismus nach der grammatisch - historischen Interpretationsmethode und nach einer freimüthigen Stellung in die (sic) vergleichende Universalgeschichte der Religionen und in die universale Religion, vol. i. (Erlangen 1813), pp. 96 ff., 120 f.

2. Kritische Geschichte der Religionsideen des A. T., vol. ii. (Berlin 1829); cf. vol. i. p. 437, for his complete view of the religious development of Israel.

3. Die Genesis historisch-kritisch erläutert (1835), p. lxi. ff.

4. Die älteren judischen Feste mit einer Kritik der Gesetzgebung des Pentateuch (1835), pp. 188, 200 f., 232–234, 291 f., 304 f.

5. Die Biblische Theologie wissenschaftlich dargestellt. 1 Theil. Die Religion des A. T. nach den Kanonischen Büchern entwickelt (Berlin 1835).

6. Der Feuer und Molochdienst der alten Hebräer als urväterlicher, legaler, orthodoxer Cultus der Nation nachgewiesen (Braunschweig 1842).

7. Ghillany (Professor and Town Librarian in Nürenberg), Die Menschenopfer der alten Hebräer (1843); cf. p. 23.

8. Mythologie und Offenbarung, vol. ii. (1845 f.); Die Biblische Theologie (1853).

9. Geschichte der Religion, vol. iii. (Leipzig 1855–57).

10. Theologische Briefe an die Gebildeten der deutschen Nation, vol. i. Das alte Testament (Leipzig).

11. Abraham Kuenen (Professor of Protestant Theology in Leyden), De Godsdienst van Israël, 2 vols. (Haarlem 1869–70); Die Profeten en die Profetie onder Israel, 2 vols. (1875); and lastly (mentioning it under the title of its German translation), Volksreligion und Weltreligion (Berlin 1883). These latest views of Kuenen, even according to his own opinion, do not affect his first well-known work. To this great work we shall accordingly refer, and it will be interesting to compare the views expressed in the different works.

12. De Israëliten te Mekka van Davids tijd (Haarlem 1864). The author here holds that the sanctuary at Mecca was founded in David's time. On this supposition he traces the origin of the representative "religion

of Abraham" from the Chanifs who were before Mohammed.

13. De dienst der Baalim onder Israël (Haarlem 1864). This book is arranged on the plan followed out by Dozy in his work already referred to. This the author acknowledges in the Introduction, § 1–3. The translation by Colenso is entitled "The Worship of Baalim in Israel" (London 1865). Oort is also the author of Het Menschenopfer in Israël (1865). The views here expressed are for the most part homologated by Colenso in his work, "The Pentateuch and the Book of Joshua," Part 5 (London 1865), pp. 269–284.

14. Land follows the same course with Colenso as to Oort's views. See Der Theologisch Tijdschrift, 1868, pp. 156–170.

15. Vergelijkende Geschiedenis van de Egyptische en Mesopotamische Godsdiensten (Amsterdam). Vol. i. (1869) contains die ägyptische Religion, and vol. ii. (1872) die mesopotamischen Religionen, p. 530. Ferner Geschiedenis, etc., translated into German by F. W. T. Weber with the title Compendium der Religionsgeschichte (Berlin 1880), § 52. Of the former, Rindtorff has furnished us with a German translation. Comp. also Das Programm der Realschule zu Weimar (1883), particularly as to its treatment of the Religion of the Phœnicians, p. 3; and Hecker (Prof. in Groningen) on Die Israeliten und der Monotheismus (1879), p. 61.

16. Die Theologie der Propheten als Grundlage für die innere Entwickelungsgeschichte der israelitischen Religion (Bonn 1875), p. 19.

17. Geschichte des Volkes Israel, 1 Theil (1878), 2nd Aufl. entitled Prolegomena zur Geschichte Israel's (1883). See also the article on "Israel" in the Encyclopædia Britannica, 9th ed. vol. xiii. (1881), pp. 396–431.

18. Die Genesis des Judenthums (in Zeitschrift für die alttestamentliche Wissenschaft herausgegeben von Stade, vol. ii. 1882, pp. 94–151), p. 107, etc.

19. Die Entwickelung des altisraelitischen Priesterthums (1880), p. 125. Also Die Entwickelung des israelitischen Prophetenthums (1883), p. 2, etc.

20. Geschichte des Volkes Israel (in Allgemeine Geschichte in Einzeldarstellungen herausgegeben von Oncken), 1881, p. 43.

21. Der Mythus bei den Hebräern und seine geschichtliche Entwickelung (1876).

22. Der Ursprung des Monotheismus (1879), p. 36 ff. Comp. also Bruchmann in the Zeitschrift für Völkerpsychologie und Sprachwissenschaft, vol. xiii. (1882), p. 456.

23. Religionsphilosophie auf geschichtlicher Grundlage (1878), pp. 356–363. Comp. also the same author's criticism of Kuenen's latest work in the German Literaturzeitung (1883), No. 12.

24. Das religiöse Bewusstsein der Menschheit im Stufengang seiner Entwickelung (Berlin 1882), p. 388 f., Anm.

25. De Godsdienst, i. 5–13: Ons Standpunt.

26. This we have already done, at least so far as the faith of the O. T. is concerned, in our Offenbarungsbegriff des Alten Testaments, vol. ii. (Leipzig 1882).

27. De Godsdienst, i. p. 8.

28. So called because it regards the earlier science of Christian religion as no longer extant.

29. Vid. Stade in Gesch. des Volkes Israel, p. 12, Anm. 1.

30. We do not here speak of its literature and archæology.

THE CHIEF PRINCIPLES OF ANCIENT ISRAEL'S RELIGION.

CHAPTER I.

Was the religion of Moses also that of the majority of his people?—The answer given to this question has been generally twofold. On the one hand, it has been so asserted, nay, more than this, we are told that a right interpretation of the Old Testament favours the view, that the Mosaic faith was that certainly of the greater part, if not of the entire nation, at the time of Moses, and indeed for some time after his removal. But, on the other hand, we find it also assumed that what might be called the higher religion of Moses was from the beginning only enjoyed by a section of the people. We shall now see which of those views corresponds most with the truth of history.

1. Throughout the Old Testament we can find no passage that tells us that Israel, led by Moses from the

land of their bondage, was ignorant of God as revealed to their fathers. Was it not to Him that the people went for help; was it not under His guidance that they found a happy deliverance; and after a period of rebellion, was it not to Him that as penitents they returned? Kaiser has referred to this, *e.g.* (p. 23): " Moses in reality changed nothing in the religion of his nation in slavery;" and again (p. 61): " His God was the Egyptian, etc., fire-essence." Daumer also substantiates the same idea in his work as well as in its title, *e.g.* (p. 3): " The worship of Moloch was the faith of Abraham, Moses, Samuel, and David." Ghillany also adopts a somewhat similar view when he says (p. 44): "The idolatry which has been so severely censured is but a form of the ancient worship;" and again (p. 79): "Should the Old Testament be searched into in an unbiassed manner, no purer religion could be found in it than that of the closely-allied tribes of Canaan. This difference, however, must be acknowledged, that whereas the God of the ordinary Semitic races is Baal or Moloch, yet with the Hebrews His name is Jahveh."

The direct proofs[1] used by Daumer in support of

---

[1] The indirect proofs (found in human sacrifice, circumcision, etc.) which Daumer and Ghillany refer to, as showing that Moloch was the legally recognised God of ancient Israel, are explained later on.

his view are as follow (p. 47). From the words, "shame (הבּשֶׁת) hath devoured the labour of our fathers from our youth . . . against Jahveh, our God, have we sinned" (Jer. iii. 24 f.), he draws the inference "of a truth that God whom the prophet set forth by the name Jahveh was never the God of Israel. Rather, we should say, it was the idol which he contrasted with Him, and called Baal and Moloch" (Jer. xi. 13, xxxii. 35). This inference, however, resembles the general rashness of his reasoning, extracting, as it does, conclusions not warranted by the text. No doubt if we only possessed the former part of the passage referred to, we might be able to accept Daumer's conclusion. But what of the latter part, referring to Jahveh in distinct terms as the peculiar God of Israel? Another point against accepting such an interpretation is the fact that Daumer himself (p. 109) in his treatment of Jer. vii. 31 says: "Such assertions that Jahveh did not wish, and had not commanded, all these sacrifices to be made, were unnecessary, nay, even absurd, if they had not been directed against an opinion prevalent in Israel which affirms what the prophet denies. . . . If man only believed that it was Jahveh's will that children should be burned on the idolatrous altars, this of itself would be regarded as nothing less than a representation of Jahveh." He cites also Vatke, who (p. 355) thus writes : " From the antithesis of Jeremiah (vii. 31, xix. 5), we may perhaps conclude that the idolatrous nation knowingly united their sacrifices of human offerings to Moloch with the worship of Jahveh, and in doing so saw no glaring apostasy." How irrelevant! Man goes on his way on his own responsibility, determines to speak, nay, has even a right to do so!

"Therefore," concludes Daumer, "the assertions of the prophet Amos (v. 25 f.), as if with one blow, shatter the framework of our general view of theology." Meantime, notwithstanding Steiner,[1] Bredenkamp,[2] and Oehler,[3] the most recent authorities, as we have already pointed out in our Thesis of 1879,[4] we must join with this that interpretation [5] which (ver. 26) refers to the future.

---

[1] *Vid.* 4th edition of Hitzig's Commentar zu den Kleinen Propheten, 1881.

[2] Gesetz und Propheten, 1881, p. 83 ff.

[3] Theologie des A. T., 1882, § 26. 4.

[4] The second dissertation, De Criticæ Sacræ argumento e linguæ legibus repetito, p. 63 : ונשאתם, Amos v. 26, ex imperativo et imperfecto versuum 23, s. explicandum est.

[5] *Vid.* Ernst Meier in his ingenious and able criticism of the works of Daumer and Ghillany in the Theolog. Studien und Kritiken, 1843, pp. 1007-1053. He mentions also his predecessors, p. 1032 f. In more recent times, Schrader, in the Theolog. Studien und Kritiken, 1874, pp. 324-332, defends our present interpretation and regards it as settled. *Vid.* the 2nd edition of Keilinschriften und A. T., 1883, p. 442.

For it is a grammatical impossibility for the interrogative sentence in ver. 25, which requires a negative answer, to be directly joined with ver. 26, an affirmative clause. This sentence, notwithstanding its present copulative form, must of necessity become an interrogative one. It is a sentence of ridicule, and clearly it seems a logical impossibility, in the interpreting of this passage, to add a purely affirmative sentence to the interrogation in ver. 25. An equally important consideration, which decides the question for itself, is the weighty fact that for a perfect understanding of the passage, ver. 26 cannot be joined to ver. 27 by "and." Moreover, "and" at the beginning of vers. 27 and 26 would lead us to infer that והגליתי (ver. 27) is the perfectum consecutivum, and therefore dependent on the future in ver. 26, and also that ונשאתם (ver. 26) is the perfectum consecutivum which would make it dependent on the imperfect of ver. 24 and the imperative of ver. 23. Ver. 25, however, comes in between with its interrogation by no means impossible or out of place, which should simplify for the readers the understanding of ver. 24: "But let judgment run down as waters, and righteousness as a mighty stream." It, however, explains the possibility of this judgment by pointing to the cessation of worship, and thus removes the expected objections. But, secondly, Daumer, with his conception of ver. 26 as a perfectum, was not entitled to ascribe to the prophet the idea that Israel during their desert life were ignorant of Jahveh (*e.g.* vers. 20, 27). For Meier has justly remarked in his work already quoted, p. 1031: "'The sacrifices' and not the term 'to me' (ל) are by the use of the interrogation regarded with greater stress;" and "Amos wishes to make manifest (vers. 21-24) that 'Jahveh' did not desire their sacrifices." Daumer also repeats, though in vain (p. 49): "With such weighty testimonies of the prophets we must deal in earnest, and it is a disgrace, resting not only on history, but the power of genius, that stress has not been laid on this long ago. Our age, however, has already begun to attach to these expressions their intrinsic value (*vid.* Vatke, p. 191), and in doing so to lay the foundations of an altogether modern O. T. history of Israel."

Daumer (p. 66 f.) is also not unmindful of the passages in Ezekiel (xvi. 1 ff., xx. 4 ff., xxiii. 1 ff.). But, on the one hand, as no one will be inclined to question the fact of this prophet having ascribed[1] to Israel leaving Egypt a certain disposition to idolatry,

[1] Comp. *e.g.* Ezek. xx. 8.

so, on the other, may we equally assert that surely no one will charge him with speaking of the Mosaic age as one without the knowledge of the revealed God. At least we can affirm, from the historical glimpses we have of Ezekiel's consciousness, the identity or oneness of his God with that of Moses. But, we may ask, who will be constrained to construct the religious history of Israel, when this consciousness, possessed not only by the prophet but by his followers, has been so little referred to?[1]

2. We are now told by the opponents of those who believe that the great part of Israel had shared along with Moses his lofty conception of God,—*e.g.* Gramberg (vol. i. p. 436 ff.), Vatke,[2] etc.,—that the apostasy of Israel in the wilderness, and following upon that, their idolatry in Canaan, are for us unintelligible, nay, even impossible, if the Israel of Moses' time had accepted a higher grade of religious development. What contradictory statements one sometimes finds not even

---

[1] As opposed to Ghillany's views, ibid. p. 27 f.; comp. Dillmann, Ueber den Ursprung der alttestl. Religion (1865), p. 5 f.; Herm. Schultz, Bibl. Theologie des A. T. (1878), cap. ix. 2, 11; Oehler, § 26, 4; Kurtz, Geschichte des Alten Bundes, ii. pp. 40 f., 418-421.

[2] Pp. 181-183, *e.g.* 183: "An individual can certainly by error and weakness fall to a lower grade, but an entire nation could hardly do so, if it had at all realized in its living form the consciousness of the spirituality and unity of God."

B

resting on a sufficient basis! Is it not possible, we would ask, that Israel wandered away from the higher conception of God they formerly possessed to something lower and more sensual? And may we not find facts sufficient in themselves to prove the accuracy of this old historical belief? For, in reality, was not Israel easily turned aside to new ideas of God, and to another worship totally different from that of their early days? Did they not turn aside to the worship of the gods of Canaan[1] as well as to those of Moab and Ammon, as they afterwards worshipped the queen and starry hosts of heaven?[2] In other words, do we not find that Israel, when brought into closer contact with other nations and with their more widely extended

---

[1] Comp. Smend, Zeitschrift für die alttestl. Wissenschaft (1882), p. 107, Anm.

[2] The warning given against worshipping "all the host of heaven" (Deut. iv. 19, xvii. 3) we may regard from the context as fixed in the Assyrian periods of Israel's history (*circa* 770 ff.). On this Riehm is right, die Gesetzgebung Mosis im Lande Moab (1854), p. 23. And it is impossible with Kleinert to find only in the passages mentioned an ancient "Sabäismus." *Vid.* his Das Deuteronomium und der Deuteronomiker (1872), pp. 109–113. Because the worship "of all the host of heaven" is a new and characteristic form of star-worship, viz. that following the worship of the stars on the basis of the more ancient star personification (Baal and Astarte). This seems to have been adopted by Israel at the time of the great growth of Assyrian power (2 Kings xvii. 16, xxi. 3, 5, xxiii. 4 f.; 2 Chron. xxxiii. 3; Jer. viii. 2; Zeph. i. 5), if the "Melecheth" of heaven, *i.e.* the moon, is not mentioned in Deuteronomy (Jer. vii. 18, xliv. 17 ff.).

political relations, were led first of all readily to accept the religion of the Canaanites among whom they sojourned, and afterwards, as they came to know them, to worship the gods of the neighbouring nations?[1] And has not even more remote Israel, without doubt, in such turnings aside, allowed themselves to be influenced by the debasing customs of the Canaanites?[2] Thus, in the gradual enlargement of her Pantheon, Israel has even before the exile made such progress, and has generally shown itself so disposed to adopt new religious customs, that we can hardly regard it as difficult to understand—and certainly it is far from being impossible—how Israel at one time possessed a certain religious level, having thus the knowledge of God, which in later days it departed from.[3]

3. Accordingly, the tradition of the Old Testament brings out the fact, that the contemporaries of Moses, as a whole, acknowledged one God,—the God of the fathers,—whom Moses as His herald and instrument

---

[1] I notice that Cäsar von Lengerke (Kenaan, Volks und Religionsgeschichte Israels (1844), p. 552 f.) has already drawn attention to this with reference to Ezek. xvi. 15-29.

[2] Riehm supports this in the article "Unzucht" of his Handwörterbuchs des Bibl. Alterthums, p. 1701.

[3] I do not require to show from Kuenen, Wellhausen, etc., that even according to their views the Nabiismus of the Canaanites had spread itself among the Israelites. Comp., on the other hand, my Offenbarungsbegriff des A. T., i. pp. 57 ff., 63 ff.

had been sent to proclaim. Yet along with this historical tradition, we do not find it asserted in the Old Testament that the contemporaries of Moses were equal to him in ability to understand their religious beliefs, or even to comprehend the primary truths of their faith.[1] But it also does not in reality affirm, that the memory of God, as the God of their fathers, was recalled to the heads of the families in Moses' time, that they might be convinced of the divine mission of Moses, and be made to recognise in their remarkable rescue a special remedy provided by the God of their fathers.[2]

[1] Perhaps some one would find from Dillmann's words sufficient grounds to doubt the accuracy of the Old Testament tradition: "To find out the new materials of religious knowledge does not belong to every man, although religiously inclined. It is confined alone to those occupying a lofty spiritual position," etc. (ibid. p. 28).

[2] This view of the Old Testament is not accepted by von Lengerke (Kenaan, pp. 376-383), although, in my judgment, he has used too strong language in speaking of "the idolatrous condition of Israel chosen by God through His servant Moses."

Ancient Israel's Religion.

CHAPTER II.

But we now ask, not simply what was the religion of the majority of the people, but what was the legally appointed religion of Israel in pre-prophetic times?[1]—If we are carefully to examine into the beliefs of more ancient Israel, we must on no account regard the idea of God merely of the majority of Israel at Moses' time as the beginning of the development of the religion of Israel. We are bound to look to the ideal religion itself, in its own nature and forms of worship. For such a true religious system could have existed in Moses' time, even although it had not found favour with the majority of his contemporaries. This we may regard as certain. And not only so, but we see how the religion of the prophets existed and so influenced

[1] By "pre-prophetic" times we are to understand that period in Israel's religious history preceding written prophecy. It also includes the period to about 800 B.C. In this arrangement the spiritual unity of all Israel's prophets is seen. But regarding this comp. my detailed representation in Offenbarungsbegriff des A. T., i. pp. 65-71, etc.

them notwithstanding the general unbelief of the nation. The weighty and deep religious and ethical views expressed in their prophetical writings would doubtless suffer neglect at the hands of those inattentive to spiritual matters, as well as of the rebellious majority of the nation. And, therefore, that religion of pre-prophetic Israel must be brought out by careful research. In the approbation found in this belief the soul of the ancient Israelite was gladdened, while the denial of this wounded his conscience. It was in the discharge of religious duty that he knew himself to be one with the old heroes of his race, united to them by inseparable ties. Joyfully he turned his eye towards heaven, and hopefully into the future. In possession of this religious belief he recognised, in his nation, the people favoured by Heaven, chosen by God; and he heartily contemned all outward and erroneous ideas of God. The loss of such a religion with its accompanying privileges seemed nothing less to him than the loss of Paradise; and, it was in the defence of this religion as a lofty idea, that his soul was so filled with glowing ardour and holy zeal. Therefore we must place the consciousness of God at the very beginning of Israel's history, from which the entire Old Testament has derived its deep signification.

It alone expresses the thanksgivings of grateful Israel in the enjoyment of God's favour, while it alone is the comprehensible answer of Israel, with thankful hearts, experiencing God's care.

In addition to this we must clearly have before our minds the idea of God prevalent in Israel at the beginning of its national existence, as well as Israel's fidelity and gratitude to God, if we are at all to understand the general history of that people in later times. This even de Wette, as we shall see, has acknowledged in his article on Vatke's work.[1] These sentences to which we refer are at the conclusion of his article, and, expressing as they do certain fixed principles by which Old Testament criticism must always be directed, they ought not to pass unnoticed. He says: "Vatke has done not a little to further the progress of development. Much that is now accepted has been sanctified by tradition, and much is received on the ground of its intrinsic worth.[2] But, moreover," and this to our mind is the most important of all, "the Hebrew people have this outstanding peculiarity, that from the beginning of their career we can trace in their midst

[1] Theologische Studien und Kritiken, 1837, pp. 947–1003.
[2] This expression of de Wette's has reference to the fact that Vatke regarded Moses as occupying the same position with his contemporaries.

the working of conscience as we do in no other nation. And this conscience is evil, testifying of feelings of guilt. It shows us also how high was the position, with its corresponding duties, which the nation enjoyed from which it neither can nor will be separated, and it reveals to our minds the dissension and struggle between knowledge as contained in the law and the will. In this struggle we see how sin increases and how frequently we witness it at work (Rom. v. 20). But according to Vatke's ideas of a natural development, this feeling does not come so often before us. It is only at certain times and amidst important events, when, *e.g.*, we regard a definite act of will, or a giving of the law, that development is at all understood and its progress denoted. And it is then that the struggle already referred to may be said to begin, and the peculiar disposition and working of the Hebrew inner life may be witnessed." Now, if such an opinion be opposed, it can only be on one ground, and that merely in questioning, if de Wette has regarded the giving of the law as the starting-point in the inner spiritual life of the people. For certainly these words imply a satisfactory hypothesis set forth by de Wette characterizing the activity of Jewish life, an experience common to Moses and his contemporaries, containing a recognition of a revealed God, a decision, as it were, coming into being about the time of their rescue, faithfully to honour God as high above all the deities of Egypt. But it is a matter beyond controversy that a consciousness of God had existed among the earliest Israelites—the God who had rescued them from bondage by a strong hand and outstretched arm, and as if on eagle's wings had brought them to Himself. God was to Israel all in all—as the soul which regulates the pulsations of moral and religious life. For all the great master-spirits of old Israel regarded themselves not as beginners, but as restorers of a condition of life seen in its most perfect form at the commencement of the national existence.[1] And, it must not withal be forgotten that the best representatives of the nation were really compelled by their own consciousness and the recollection of the people solely to dedicate themselves to the list of reformers, notwithstanding the warmth of their zeal and the energy of their own wills. As such they were enabled to recall the faithfulness of God to the nation's recollection, and to exhort men to a life of allegiance to Him (Isa. i. 2 f.; Jer. viii. 10-13, etc.). And it is as a consequence of this that the faith of pre-prophetic Israel rested upon

[1] *Vid.* Hos. xi.

so firm a basis, cherished and preserved inviolate by the pious hearts of ancient Israel who still adhered to the historical, as well as to their own religious, consciousness of God.

CHAPTER III.

This lawful religion of the pre-prophetic Israel, furthermore, from a formal point of view, represented the ideas of God possessed by Moses, the pious of Israel, and at the same time the working and writing prophets. —It is generally supposed that the spirit of the writing prophets has been always akin to that of the best among the more ancient representatives of Israel. And this must be accepted, in so far at least as it is not condemned by these prophets themselves. For it rests not simply on the negative grounds already mentioned (*vid.* under Chap. II.), but it is positively proved that these writing prophets unite with the old religious heroes of the nation, and together they seek to revive a relative development of religious progress among their people.

Not to speak of Noah (Ezek. xiv. 14, 20 ; Isa. liv. 9) and his "righteousness," the writing prophets place their hope in Abraham and Jacob, because it was to them that God, with an oath, had promised to be faithful and gracious (Micah vii. 20 ; comp. Jer. xxxiii. 26 ; Ezek. xxxiii. 24 ; Ps. cv. 6). Abraham they regarded as the "friend of their God" (Isa. xli. 8), and they recognised in Jacob the channel through which God had communed with their nation (Hos. xii. 4). Furthermore, Moses is not so seldom mentioned by these writing prophets as Ghillany[1] endeavours to make out. No doubt it is true, but only in a formal manner, what von der Alm has said with such emphasis (p. 179): "Micah is the only one of the prophets living before the year 622 who has spoken of Moses."[2] For Hosea (xii. 3) says: "By a prophet the Lord brought Israel out of Egypt, and by a prophet were they preserved." There the prophet has evidently Moses in his mind, just also as Jeremiah writes (vii. 25): "Since the day that your fathers came forth out of the land of Egypt unto this day, I have even sent unto you all my servants the

---

[1] In his work already quoted, p. 27 : "A weighty fact not, in my estimation, sufficiently regarded is this, that the name of Moses does not appear in any prophet, except the post-exilian Malachi (iv. 4) and Daniel (ix. 11, 13). I at least do not find this name mentioned in the prophets."

[2] He will, concerning this, regard the interrogatory statement of Micah as an interpolation, in order to determine this pre-Josian mention of Moses.

prophets." And to these we must add the two passages in Micah vi. 4 and Isa. lxiii. 11, where Moses is specially referred to.

But over and above these direct quotations from the prophetical writings regarding Moses, we find that the oldest prophets regard themselves as the general possessors of a law by which the ethical and religious movements of Israel were to be regulated. This is beyond question, even without maintaining the old representation[1] that Moses was the author of the Pentateuch. For the prophets knew of a Torah which formed the standard code of duty in the minds

[1] Comp. the grounds of this negation in my Offenbarungsbegriff des A. T., ii. pp. 321-332. Since then, Driver in the Journal of Philology, vol. xi. (1882) pp. 201-233, has tried to rob Giesebrecht's proof of its peculiar force and decided power. But it is clear, p. 232, in reference to אנכי and אני that he has not altogether succeeded. His method of proof is, moreover, unmethodical; comp. e.g. p. 209, what he says of ילד and הוליד, where he does not from first to last sufficiently unfold the progressive nature of the forms of speech. On the other hand, Maybaum in his treatise, "Zur Pentateuchkritik" (Zeitschrift für Völker-psychologie und Sprachwissenschaft, 1883, pp. 191-202), has not sufficiently proved to my mind that language contains no authoritative proof. Böhl (Zum Gesetz und Zeugniss, 1883) and Pressel (Geschichte und Geographie der Urzeit, 1883) in their criticisms on the literary aspects of the question have not sufficiently estimated the proof derived from language; and lastly, Roos (Die Geschichtlichkeit des Pentateuchs, etc., 1883) acknowledges (p. 166): "We did not intend to point out by our investigation that the ecclesiastical view which maintains the authenticity of the Pentateuch and its historical law-giving is not in the light of history the only one possible, and, therefore, of necessity to be accepted by all."

of the Israelites, peculiar in itself, and different from the individual commands of Jahveh sent forth from time to time as the vicissitudes of Israel demanded.[1] Moreover, Amos begins his condemnation of the two tribes with the words (ii. 4): "For three transgressions of Judah and for four, I will not turn away the punishment thereof; because they have despised the law of the Lord, and have not kept His commandments." Now it cannot be considered as settled that the prophet in the use of his expression (חקים) had referred to a fixed law given by God.[2] And for him who will create a history of religion from the material supplied by its own sources and not according to his own preconceived ideas, the second and third chapter of this Book of Amos are peculiarly fitted to describe the chief relationship between written prophecy and the further development of Israel. For, in these chapters we not only find the existence of a moral code supposed, according to which the oppression of the poor meets with fitting condemnation (ii. 6–8), but the prophet recognises in himself the guardian

---

[1] *Vid.* the decision regarding this important point given in detail in my Offenbarungsbegriff des A. T., ii. pp. 334 f., 343–349.

[2] The writings of the Old Testament, not directly proceeding from the prophets, have also correctly ascribed to Moses a high place among the instruments used for the divine revelation (Ex. xxxiii. 11; Num. xii. 6–8; Deut. xxxiv. 10).

of the nation's most sacred memories (ii. 9, 10). And, moreover, he was the supporter of the despised Nazarites and prophets (ii. 11, 12), and, along with this, he was a member of that royal community whose business it is to proclaim God according to the real and verbal manifestations vouchsafed to them (iii. 19).

So little difference therefore do we find in the fundamentals of their religion between the prophets whose writings have come down to us, and those other so-called prophets of action, as there is between the prophets generally and the priesthood.[1] This at least can be seen with reference to the representation of God. For these peculiarities of the priesthood can only be understood in the light of the general worship. Last of all we find this to be the case, when we remember that David is spoken of by Amos, not simply once with contempt as the player on the harp (vi. 5),[2] but as the honoured and blessed founder of Israel's royal house (ix. 11). From such facts we are able to see that already the oldest prophets saw in David the prince chosen of God by special favour,

---

[1] I only mention, *e.g.*, the priest Uriah, the witness of Isaiah (viii. 2).

[2] Against Vatke, who (p. 293) has founded his decisions on these passages of Amos, the songs of David can hardly describe the ruling religious tendencies because they first presupposed a later age.

and in this they recognised themselves at one with Nathan (2 Sam. vii.). And they acknowledged that this saying of Nathan had been at times reproduced, *e.g.* by David himself (2 Sam. xxiii. 1-7), as well as by other poets (Ps. ii., lxxxix., etc.).

Thus by negative as well as positive arguments it has been shown that the opinion (frequently expressed in different ways by the Theorists of Development)[1] about the writing prophets having introduced changes into the appointed religion of Israel is certainly groundless. This can almost be proved from an *à priori* point of view, but it is better to regard it as resting on the grounds of formal right.

The importance of the formal argument, which we must now treat of, for the identity of the pre-prophetic period with that of the prophetic, in their respective views of God, is not to be underestimated. And it is somewhat enhanced by the fact that although, in looking back, the exercise of an arbitrary spirit was shown by the prophets in the discharge of those

---

[1] To show that the religion of Israel had been altogether changed in form since about the year 700, Ghillany (p. 50 f.) ventures to assert: "The commencement of an attempted purifying of religion was made in Palestine somewhere about the same time as it was in Media through Zoroaster," and that "the prophet Jeremiah, occupying as he does such a high position above his contemporaries, with regard to his religious views, is a firm friend of the Chaldeans."

judicial functions which they assumed towards their fellow-countrymen, yet, the assertion might be made that the extent of this formal position, which has been already explained, was limited. For as with the ancients generally, so was it the case with the Israelites and the prophets in particular, that no regard was paid to historical development, and at the same time no great interest taken in the existence of things. By such a statement the opportunity is only given us to convict those making it of what might be called a general and then a special error. In so doing we permit the force of the previous distinctions to appear for the first time with their full weight.

Firstly, Have we not noticed that the historical books of the Old Testament, in several instances, have notified the commencement of certain forms of worship or changes in them? Such are their statements, for example, on the origin of nomad life, the founders of music, and of working in metals (Gen. iv. 20–22, etc.).[1] But, secondly, how accurate is the description given in these annals of Israel's religious history, with its periods of progress and its many backslidings! Now, even limiting ourselves to

---

[1] *Vid.* the complete list of passages in my Offenbarungsbegriff des A. T., i. p. 164.

such facts, we see that Israel has always regarded the period of Moses' activity as a time of great historical progress, and, in so doing, it finds in the destruction of the patriarchal system, with the rearing of that given by Moses in its place, a phase of development. For, with the person of Moses there was always associated the knowledge of a new divine name,[1] and at the same time the idea of a new law [2] with its religious and ethical claims. And no one, indeed, can gainsay the fact that Israel generally looked upon Moses as the founder of all its religious customs, just as we find other nations regarding some illustrious soul with feelings of veneration and esteem. Moreover, going farther back, we see in what high estimation Jacob and still more Abraham were regarded by the Israelites. As they were the earthly, so were they also the spiritual fathers of their nation; those who had originated and exemplified for the nation that high pattern of individual life. If, therefore, it be correctly asserted that Israel can go back into the past for the origin of its ideal life, begun in some capricious moments, and not

---

[1] The recognition of the Tetragramm (יהוה) being the best sign of God who had joined Himself to men.

[2] The constitution of the stipulations of union.

resting on a historical basis, we can only say that Israel must have derived the higher beginnings of its national life from its oldest heroes at various unknown periods.

And, further, Israel with its pretended lack of historical understanding has, on the other side, not allowed itself to be misled. For, while it regards the time of Moses as the only great period, so it looks upon the period following as one altogether different. In fact, the whole history after Moses' time is one of continual backslidings. Israel has thus a knowledge of its true history, and, moreover, it has been careful faithfully to preserve that knowledge. And thus we find that it was between Abraham and Moses that the high standpoint was reached in the views possessed of God.[1] These more fully revealed by Moses were

---

[1] The significance of this fact has been partially brought out by Maybaum when he says in Die Entwickelung des Israelitischen Prophetenthums (1883): "The claims made by the Biblical narrative for a high grade of Mosaic systems being found in the patriarchs only show us that they had in mind a sort of development." But this is done in a most general manner, and is opposed by frequent traces of Israel's understanding of history. If it can be accepted (comp. Wurster in der Zeitschrift für die alttestl. Wissenschaft (1884), p. 127 f.), we find a Jewish historian dividing the elements of the revealed religion, superior as they were to those of the heathen faith, into the pre-Sinaitic and Sinaitic periods. The division is wrought out on an à priori theory, but it rests on unsatisfactory grounds.

faithfully adhered to in the conceptions of generations, and finally expressed in writing. But in addition to this, amidst all their political changes, we find that Israel always regarded, in its striking connections, the spread of apostasy; and such times of falling away, with the persons responsible for bringing on the moral darkness of these centuries, were by no means forgotten.

In opposition, however, to this general and much observed truth as to Israel having preserved the memories of the many changes which had passed over its national life,—and this record, be it remembered, is kept in full precision and with historical minuteness,[1]— yet, first of all, we have not inquired if the primitive and patriarchal history employed in the pre-Mosaic times the name "Jahveh"—chosen by God in the time of Moses as His own peculiar name. And following upon this we have not seen if the later sources of post-Mosaic history have employed a more recently fixed ideal in their understanding of the divine revelations.[2] We must, however, remember that in the use of the name

---

[1] Comp. p. 18.

[2] The first formal claim for the unity of a fixed form of divine worship is in Deuteronomy.

"Jahveh" by pre-Mosaic history, no alteration was intended in the religious memories of Israel; because the Jahvist (Ex. iii. 1 ff.) as well as the Elohist (vi. 2 f.) adopt the name of God by which He had revealed Himself to Moses instead of the term Jahveh. And the critic of Deuteronomy, in treating of post-Mosaic history, does not assert that this fixed form of worship had existed from Moses' time. He only complains that the kings, after the building of Solomon's Temple (1 Kings iii. 2), had not yet comprehended the ideal of this special form of worship, which would have been easily preserved by true and faithful priests. Finally, if such criticism of Deuteronomy has even dated back to Moses' time the tendency to centralize the divine worship, there must have been first of all no prophet, while at the same time we have to acknowledge that a prophet was blamed for changing Jahveh's law (Jer. viii. 8). Moreover, the prophets cannot be charged with these corresponding deviations from tradition. But, secondly, along with this centralization of worship, notwithstanding its ideal aim, the protection of particular interests on the part of the priests at Jerusalem played as important a part. This was to keep off idolatrous tendencies by priestly control. It seems to us, however, that we need only defend the position,[1] with regard to the certainty of Israel's history, which claims that the Old Testament traditions in their various characteristics, and in those parts affecting the nation, must be considered as resting on satisfactory bases. To support this fundamental position there are three grounds from which the accuracy of the ancient Jewish tradition must necessarily be found. These are—(*a*) We find in Israel manifold traces showing us that oral tradition from generation to generation was maintained in great force (comp. my Offenbarungsbegriff des A. T., i. p. 164). (*b*) Israel possessed, at a comparatively early period, its past history recorded in writing, *e.g.* the Ten Words, the Book of the Covenant, which corresponds with the oldest phase of Israel's religious history, etc. Then we have the historical songs, beginning with that recorded in the 15th chapter of Exodus; and, further, we have the Song of Deborah, which, according to Stade (*vid.* Geschichte, p. 49), "is wanting in its direct impressions of the songs of victory as these were generally sung," etc. (*c*) No principle, or starting-point in history, can be discovered by which, or when, Israel could have invented the essential features of its national tradition,

---

[1] Comp. my "Beiträge zur Biblischen Chronologie," in the Zeitschrift für kirchliche Wissenschaft und kirchliches Leben, 1883, p. 281.

e.g. the calamitous but victorious march out of Egypt.[1] Thirdly, in dealing with this question there comes before us, not merely the possibility of the prophets having abolished the ancient historical recollections of the people, but also the possibility that they had destroyed the religious and ethical consciousness of their hearers, peculiar as that was to each according to their respective condition. Thus they did not merely conceal the novelty of their views, but reckoning them as ancient, made them to be considered with respect, and on these fictitious grounds they claimed for themselves the position of those proclaiming the law, and even at the same time, executors of justice. Moreover, the prophets have not only marked where they stand in antithesis towards the false, but they show the divine and Mosaic derivation of the particularized legal worship (Amos v. 21 ff., etc.), and they have also expressly asserted where they condemn any propositions made by man (*vid.* Jer. xxxi. 29 ; Ezek. xviii. 1 ff.).

[1] Stade, in his Geschichte Israels, does not go so far as either Seinecke (Geschichte Israels, i. p. 1) or Popper (ibid. pp. 98, 121, 126 ff.) in denying the historical basis of the ancient tradition of Israel. Still he also goes so far as to say (p. 129): "If once a Hebrew clan did exist in Egypt, no one knows its name." But Smend in the Zeitschrift für die alttestl. Wissenschaft, 1882, p. 119, and also Wellhausen in his article "Israel," in the Encyclopædia Britannica, xiii. p. 400 f., regard, and rightly so, the exodus from Egypt as the starting-point of the history of Israel.

For these reasons it cannot be regarded as possible that the proof, afforded us by consideration of such negative and positive arguments, has been confuted. By them the moral and religious bases of prophetical preaching have been for the common good of the Israel faithful in its allegiance to Jahveh. Accordingly, we consider it to be our duty to the principle which holds that the unanimous teaching of the Old Testament, even on a single point, can only be robbed of the authority attached to it by most convincing reasons, to take up and to vindicate the greatest possible distance between Kuenen, along with his predecessors and followers. In so doing we would call to mind the fact that Kuenen himself once announced this principle referred to with regard to the significance of the historical consciousness of Israel.[1]

---

[1] De Godsdienst, i. pp. 397-401. Comp. the translation of the interesting sentence at p. 34.

CHAPTER IV.

Collection of the formal views, and the transition to the material inquiries. — The writing prophets about the year 700 have given, and indeed spread, the views held in common by them regarding God; and these views they regarded as the only legitimate. Now, in the actual history of religion in Israel, and not in any capricious treatment of it either in its gloomy aspects, can we find one of those prophetical representations, deviating from the general idea of God, still cherished in its living form in Israel? The answer to such an inquiry is as follows: That all the existing differences between the religion of the pre-prophetical Israel, and that indeed of the people generally on the one hand, and the religion of the prophets on the other, must be regarded as a return of part of the nation, greater or smaller as the case may be, to the religious condition of the time preceding Abraham or even Moses. Such backslidings would be brought about partly by human frailty,[1] and partly by the inclination, springing from selfishness and sensuality,[2] to worship the gods of their neighbours, at hand or far off as these may be. This is made clear to us in the general views of the prophets and in the national literature, as well as in the general consciousness [3] of the people.

Thus, so far as the Israel of the prophetical period, or the time near that, fell away from the appointed religion of Israel, maintained as that was by the prophets, we must conclude, *e.g.* with Amos (ii. 4)[4] and Hosea (ii. 15), that Israel had left its proximity to God, which it had enjoyed in Abraham and Moses, and had gone far from God. In doing so, they had left the God who is a Spirit, and who specially regards the spiritual element in man, for the service of idols, whose forms are always visible to the eye, while the worship they demand at the hands of the devotee is sensual.

---

[1] Matt. xxvi. 41.

[2] So with Paul (Gal. v. 19-21). Out of selfishness is seen this first side of the active σάρξ—the εἰδωλολατρεία: "They serve the creature instead of the Creator" (Rom. i. 25). The worship of the Canaanites, with its concessions to lewdness, forms the second side to the active σάρξ, *i.e.* sensuality.

[3] Concerning this I have already written a treatise, which I hope to publish this year in the Zeitschrift für kirchliche Wissenschaft und kirchliches Leben.

[4] Josh. xxiv. 2, 14 ; Hos. ii. 13.

But, moreover, we hope to be able to prove by a true exegesis of the Old Testament that most of these events in the traditional history of Israel, regarded by the theorists on development as so many traces of a lower and higher development in the pre-prophetical and prophetical periods of Israel's religious history,[1] are only visionary. For anew we shall hope to prove according to a correct, we mean by that the general, view of the Old Testament representation of the passages concerned, that neither the pretended traces of the (earlier) physical idea of God altogether exclude the ethical, nor *vice versa* is the ethical idea of God (of later days) without its physical background. And we hope to bring to the clear and calm recollection of our readers the chief points of the development theory in opposition to the judgment of the prophetical, and indeed non-prophetical authors, showing that these declarations of the Old Testament, in which special revelation has not been recognised as a departure from the moral and religious prerogatives of the people, form in reality but two poles of one and the same revelation.

---

[1] *E.g.* I take as a proof of a lower grade of development in Israel's views of God, the appearances of God as a destroying fire (Ex. xxiv. etc.; Kuenen, De Godsdienst, i. p. 240); and as a pretended proof in such sayings as Isa. x. 17, where holiness is said to become Jahveh, of the higher phase of development found in the eighth century B.C.

Accordingly, our views by no means correspond with those who hold so strongly by development, to whom we would say: The development of Israel, so questionable, proves itself as a reality only in part, while it presents itself far more as something visionary. For the reality that lies before us is the divine representation, or the sinful backslidings and idolatries.

In undertaking the last part of the proof already referred to, we shall answer in due course the following questions :—

CHAPTER V.

What development can we trace in the name of Israel's lawful God?—So far as the name of the pre-prophetical God is concerned, says Daumer, it may be the same as Chiun (*i.e.* Saturn, *vid.* Amos v. 26),[1] as Molech,[2] and, finally, from an older יהוה, with "which,

---

[1] Comp. the correct interpretation of this passage already given.

[2] Daumer, ibid. p. 112 ff., does not merely conclude from Solomon's friendship with the Phœnicians, and from 2 Chron. xv. 8, which speaks only of repairing the altar, that the altar for burnt-offerings in Solomon's temple was an image of the ox-headed Molech, but also from 2 Sam. xii. 31: "David made the Ammonites pass through במלבן," he tells us that David was a worshipper of Molech. And Daumer would have been obliged to refer to this passage (if he regards the Kethib as correct) for the purpose of proving that Molech was the national god of the Ammonites, to whom prisoners taken in war by Ammon were to be sacrificed. (Regarding the Qeri, comp. Hofmann in the Zeitschrift für die alttestl. Wissenschaft, 1882, p. 66.) But Daumer ventures still further to suppose that David, on account of his connection with the worship of Molech, had bought the place of sacrifice from the Canaanitish priest Araria, instead of simply removing this enemy and taking his property. Daumer also does not consider (p. 129 f.) the comparison of 2 Sam. viii. 15 ff., 1 Kings iv. ff., 1 Chron. xviii. 14, sufficient ground for concluding that, firstly, in the older conditions of divine worship in Israel priestly offices are exceptionally

when compared with הוה, *howa, howwa* (destruction, annihilation), the signification 'who will destroy,' is connected" (p. 11). Daumer, however, is not so sceptical with regard to the time when Israel began to call its God by the Tetragrammaton, as von Bohlen, who in his work already referred to, p. civ., ventures the assertion that the name Jahveh could, at the most, have come into use in David's time. This last-mentioned writer appealed, in his argument, first of all to the thought, which seemed to him satisfactory, that Jahveh's house was regulated after the pattern of a princely palace, and only the time of royal ascendancy could have perfected this idea. Then Jahveh concealed Himself in the Holy of Holies. Like to an Eastern ruler, He had His messengers, who might be

---

filled by non-Levites; and, secondly, that כהן expressed another idea than that of priest. But he ventures the assertion that in the original texts of the passages already referred to מלך has been taken for Molech. One hears still, in going over his famous exposition of 1 Sam. xiii. (p. 128), the quintessence of pp. 131-136. As at Eli's time, the old Molech-Jehovismus had gone into the background, and a worship of quite a different spirit prevailed. This worship promoted sensuality (1 Sam. ii. 22), and was identical with the worship of Peor, which resembled the ancient Hebrew worship of an ass, Dionysius, and Water (Tac. Hist. 5. 3 f.). And it was Samuel who replaced the old orthodox worship of Molech-Jehovah. For 1 Sam. ii. 30, 35 is the speech of a king while as yet there is none. He is also there spoken of as the "anointed of Jahveh," and is to be understood as referring to Molech!!!

before Him as His servants. He allowed incense to be burnt before Him; He was jealous of other gods, and without offerings no one ventured to come into His presence. Nevertheless, it is manifest that the earnest crises of Jahveh-worship originated first of all from the idea of God and the natural relations of pious men to God, and could not in any sense be regarded as the outcome of comparison between Jahveh and the royal princes. And, secondly, such a comparison of their God with an Eastern prince, on the part of Israel, could have already been accomplished even before they possessed the earthly representative of their heavenly King. In looking back upon von Bohlen's first argument one is not compelled, nay, in our opinion we are scarcely entitled, from it, to prove that the incense-offering appears for the first time after Isaiah's day, as Wellhausen [1] asserts. According to him, the qetōreth, up to Jeremiah's time, is to be regarded only as the evaporation arising from the fat of animals sacrificed. Against this interpretation we have this fact before us, that in Isaiah (i.) the incense-offering is joined in the priestly codex (Lev. ii. 1), not with the sacrifice of animals alone (Isa. i. 11), but first of all with the Minchah and with the fruit-offering.

[1] *Vid.* Geschichte Israels, p. 68 f.; Prolegomena, p. 67

And in this connection the qetōreth appears (Isa. i. 13).

Further, von Bohlen remarked that old proper names having אל affixed to them (*e.g.* Israel, Samuel, etc.) quite disappear with and after David. And moreover, he says that such names with יהו (*e.g.* Jehonatham) come before us first of all at the time of that king, and that יהושע is simply a recognised change of הושע (salus). Now, in his remarks on these words, no doubt von Bohlen has taken up a correct position, but he has shot past the mark in his conclusion. It is, of course, true that Jahveh does not appear in proper names in pre-Mosaic times.[1] Before Samuel we find it only in the names Jokhebed (Ex. vi. 20, etc.), Jehoschua (Num. xiii. 16), a newer form of the name Hoschea given under Moses (Num. xiii. 8; Deut. xxxii. 44), Joas (father of Gideon, Judg. vi. 11), Jotham (Judg. ix. 5, 7), and, finally, Jonathan (Moses' grandson, Judg. xviii. 30). From such facts we are only entitled to adopt such views as the following:—

---

[1] We do not mention Moriah, Ahijah, Abijah, and Bihiah (Gen. xxii. 2; 2 Chron. iii.; 1 Chron. ii. 25, iv. 18). But the name of the temple, according to the narrative (נראה), originated after the partial appearing of Jahveh to David (1 Chron. xxi. 16). And so far as the other names are concerned, the narrative, in proportion as it enters into historical details, can afford no warrant for asserting that the term Jahveh was known in patriarchal times.

(*a*) In opposition to the existing Prolepsis of Jahveh's name in that part of Genesis where it is used, the Elohist has rightly refrained from the confusion of certain periods of religious history (Ex. vi. 3). (*b*) From the name of Moses' mother, if this has been correctly handed down to us,[1] although we may not gather that the name of Jahveh was already known to the patriarchs in Canaan, as Oehler-Delitzsch [2] and Herm. Schultz [3] conclude, yet God was regarded as such by the family of Moses in Egypt.[4] By Moses this name, which so exquisitely expresses [5] the faithfulness and constancy of God, had been proclaimed as the *Nomen proprium* of the revealed God. We

---

[1] I would adopt this on account of the importance of Moses' family.

[2] See article "Jehova" in the PRE², vi. (1879) p. 507.

[3] Theologie des A. T., 1878, p. 490.

[4] Regarding the origin of the name Jehova, Tholuck agrees with this view (Verm. Schriften, Gotha 1867, pp. 189-205), p. 201; and so do Ewald, Lehre der Bibel von Gott, i. (1871) p. 336 f.; Nestle, Die israelitischen Eigennamen nach ihrer religionsgeschichtlichen Bedeutung, 1876, p. 80; Friedr. Wilh. Schultz in Zöckler's Handbuch der Theolog. Wissensch. i. (1882), p. 299; Kuenen, De Godsdienst, i. p. 276, where he says: "Moses could not well have invented the name Jahveh; in all probability it was already in use in a limited circle;" and, last of all, Wellhausen, in the article "Israel," p. 397: "Jahveh was, before Moses' time, a sign for El; and this was used in Moses' family or in the tribe of Joseph."

[5] Well does Hitzig controvert the assertion that regards the derivation of Jahveh from "היה" to be incorrect. (*Vid.* Vorlesungen über Bibl. Theologie, etc. des O. T. Herausgeg. durch Kneucker, 1880, p. 37 f.)

cannot find the slightest reason to doubt the unanimous tradition attributing the sentence: "I am Jahveh, thy God," to Moses. And, moreover, the alteration of the name of Hosea, Moses' follower, to Joshua, is a certain witness of these historical recollections of Israel. For, depend upon it, had this name of God been proclaimed through another channel, that person would not have remained unknown to us. Furthermore, between Moses and Samuel there is no period of religious history in Israel unaccounted for; and, finally, the commencement of Samuel's time does not bear so much upon it the mark of productiveness as that of reformation. Accordingly, we may consider it as settled that, at least since Moses' time, the name of God as יהוה was known in Israel, so that really it was said: "I that am the Lord thy God from the land of Egypt" (Hos. xii. 9).

No doubt von Bohlen tells us with special emphasis that the older phrases, such as the oaths and proverbial sayings, are associated mostly with Elohim. But in opposition to this argument, somewhat weak, though its basis be strong, Tuch [1] has already (1838) said that the holy dread always shown before the sacred *Nomen proprium* of God is the principle by

---

[1] *Vid.* Commentar über die Genesis von Friedrich Tuch, p. xli. f.

which we are to explain Job i. 5, Lev. xxiv. 16, and the ברך אלהים in 1 Kings xxi. 10, 13. And this, he says, may have been at work, so that the popular form of the curse, first in use among the people, and latterly appearing in written form: "So may God do to me," etc. (1 Sam. iii. 17, etc.), was most often used only as a token of the heavenly power, rather than the name of God itself.

Lastly, von Bohlen appeals to the fact that in the Psalms of Korah, Elohim is almost exclusively the name by which God is mentioned. We must say that this fact does not afford important proof. For the psalms[1] referred to by von Bohlen have nothing in them specially referring to God's name, but belong to by far the larger division of psalms—which we might call the Elohim Psalms. Not even do they prove the assertion, sometimes made, that the term אלהים was that most used in the poetry of David's time.[2]

---

[1] He should have regarded these psalms as belonging to the second division or Book of Psalms.

[2] This representation of the term Elohim, which appears as a kind of supplement, e.g. in comparing Ps. xiv. with Ps. liii., we would not regard, as Delitzsch does (vid. Die Psalmen, 4 Aufl. 1883, p. 17), as a general peculiarity of that kind of poetry. Nor would we conclude with Keil (Einleitung, 1873, § 114, 2), from the conscious struggle, that it was a warning to the heathen against Israel's God being only regarded in the light of some national deity. We must

As his reasons will not therefore stand the test applied to them, we are not surprised that von Bohlen's views have obtained the support of only a few among the learned of recent times. For his position implies the calling in question of the Mosaic origin of the Tetragramm, as well as the assertion, already referred to, that the time of David and Solomon was specially characterized by the use of יהוה—a term of Egyptian origin. In due course we shall now proceed to peruse the arguments brought forward by the modern representatives of von Bohlen. Before doing so, however, perhaps we may be allowed to make the following digression, that no defects may be found in our mode of inquiry.

As the theory concerning the Tetragramm, already given by Moses, may have developed itself, and could be supported by asserting that the term Jahveh was derived from an altogether different religious system, we are constrained to give the general opinions of the scientific world[1] along with those views which specially appear to us as correct. If Israel did in

---

rather regard it as a *Nomen proprium* applied to the God of revelation, and this on the grounds of the general awe which was ever increasing and had its springs in the false transcendentalism of later centuries.

[1] Comp. Tholuck's treatise, ibid. p. 27, for the older representatives of the isolated derivations of the Tetragramm.

reality derive this idea from another nation, it could only have done so by contact, real or imaginary, with that people. Accordingly, it will best suit our purpose to inquire as to the nations likely to have known this name of Jahveh given to God.

The fact that the Indo-Germanic languages possess in Jove the name of God used by Israel, is proved by von Bohlen (Genesis, p. ciii.), Vatke (p. 672), and also by J. G. Müller[1] as "one not to be lightly regarded." Only there has been so little contact between the Indo-Germanic and Semitic languages in general, that we cannot conceive it as possible that it can be derived from the Indo-Germanic div (sig. to light), and thus become adopted into the Semitic speech. Much more probable is the supposition that this extant Jewish word, Jahveh, has derived its origin from a Semitic verb. For certainly it is not a linguistic or etymological, but rather an ideal or religious historical reference to the Indo-Germanic, which Hitzig[2] wished to defend with regard to יהוה when he said: "In all probability Jahveh has been derived from Astuads, *i.e.* Astvat, which signifies the Existing One, God being thus regarded in the Armenian tongue. It was according to this idea that Moses formed his new name for God. And he could only have done this because his mind had been prepared to grasp the idea, and he recognised the thought in astuads reflecting the truth and depth of that character which he wished to express." But how

---

[1] J. G. Müller (in Basel), Die Semiten in ihrem Verhältniss zu Chamiten und Japhethiten, Gotha 1872, p. 163.

[2] Vorlesungen über Bibl. Theologie, etc., p. 38.

can we believe that Moses while in Egypt copied this name of God from the Armenians, if the narrative of the flood mentions Ararat of Armenia (Gen. viii. 4), and if the most ancient traditions of Israel show their point of departure to have been more in the north-east than in the south?[1]

Accordingly, if an Arian or even Japhetical source of the Tetragramm seems impossible, we must accept a proto-Chaldaic origin of the (alleged) ideal of Jahveh, viz. Jau. This arises from the close and living contact which the Hebrews had with the descendants of Ham, the original inhabitants of Babylon (Gen. x. 8–12). This has at last been accepted by Friedrich Delitzsch.[2] On this point, however, we are forced to disagree with Friedrich Philippi,[3] who has shown, on the one hand, that the ideas of Delitzsch, opposed as these are to the usual interpretation of יהוה, as the Qal form of הוה, and of Jahu, Jah, Jeho, Jo, as abbreviations of that form, are unavailing; and, on the other hand, that Delitzsch's assertions about an original Jau having been re-modelled to Jahu, are impossible, and without proof; although an Assyrian-Babylonian god, Jau, may have existed, and may have possessed the name of a deity known in Accad and Sumir. The Hebrew and Assyrian origin of the name יהוה does not therefore

---

[1] On this point comp. Dillmann, Ueber die Herkunft der urgeschichtlichen Sagen der Hebräer (Sitzungsberichte du Academie der Wissenschaften zu Berlin vom 27 April 1882), pp. 12, 14.

[2] Wo lag das Paradies? (Leipzig 1881), p. 158 ff.

[3] "Ist יהוה accadisch-sumerischen Ursprungs?" Vid. Zeitschrift für Völkerpsychologie und Sprachwissenschaft, 1883, pp. 175–190.

seem at all possible, according to Schrader.[1] But did the Canaanites [2]— those descendants of Ham, who wandered from the neighbourhood of Babylon, bordering on the Red Sea into the Semitic provinces—not possess the name Jahveh in some form? If solitary traces of the name Jahveh had been found, not indeed in Κολπία, but, *e.g.*, in the name of a Hamitic king (2 Sam. viii. 10) and in cuneiform inscriptions, we may regard it on historical grounds as probable that Gentile tribes had taken the name Jahveh into the circle of their gods.[3] But again, by another separation of the descendants of Ham from the Egyptians, some wish us to regard the origin of the Tetragramm as an imitation partly in language and partly in idea. Röth [4] attempted the former of these, in that he considered Jahveh as but a fresh representation of the Moon god Joh. But then it was not known how, from among the countless gods of Egypt, Israel had chosen the well-known god Joh,

---

[1] Die Keilinschriften und das A. T., 1883, p. 25.

[2] Comp. my Historisch-kritisches Lehrgebäude der Hebr. Sprache i. (1881), p. 14 f. This idea is not confuted by Budde in Die Biblische Urgeschichte (1883), p. 329 ff.

[3] This is supported by Graf Baudissin in Studien zur Semitischen Religionsgeschichte, i. (1876), p. 223.

[4] Röth, Geschichte unserer abendländischen Philosophie, 1 Band : Die Aegyptische und die Zoroastrische Glaubenslehre (1846), note 175, towards the close : "That the Egyptian idols seem as small images of the oracle (Urim and Thummim) belonging to a Jewish high priest, is not to be looked upon as strange. Perhaps it would be more to the point to say that the whole Hebrew worship originated in Egypt, and that one of the two deities of Light, IOΒ, became the national God of the Hebrews יה, יהוה [*sic*] 'Ιαώ."

and besides יהוה[1] stands in no special connection with the moon; from which we are led to conclude that the resemblance alluded to must be regarded as a robust connection of great but dissimilar ideas. Some writers, however, wish to regard this latter hypothesis which connects the Jahveh-conception with an Egyptian idea as, in a double way, the real starting-point of the Tetragramm. Firstly, the words: "I am that I am" (Ex. iii. 14), the Old Testament definition of the Tetragramm, are said to be a translation[2] by Plutarch of an inscription on the Temple of Isis at Sais.[3] But this inscription exhibits the goddess Neith "as the eternally self-producing one, whereas Jahveh expresses an altogether different idea."[4] But, secondly, the idea expressed in Jahveh is said to be a reproduction of the Egyptian words nuk pu nuk.[5] Regarding this we

[1] Such a connection as that indicated between יהוה and the moon is not brought out in the Old Testament. Accordingly, it can do little to illustrate or prove on the basis of historical religion the relationship subsisting between יהוה and the facts in question, how that at Ur Raschin the moon deity Sin was for the most part worshipped (Hommel, Die Semitischen Völker und Sprachen, Leipzig 1838, p. 487); that the Sabæans of Harran worshipped the moon under this name "Sin" (Chevolsoher, Die Ssabier, 1856, i. p. 403 ff.), and that apparently the wilderness of Sin and Mount Sin-ai have derived their names from the Deity. (Comp. my article "Sin" in the Protest. Real-Encyclopädie, vol. xiv. (1884), pp. 279-281.)

[2] *E.g.* Voltaire, Reinhold, Schiller, etc. Comp. also Tholuck, ibid. pp. 189-193.

[3] De Iside, cap. 9: Τὸ ἐν Σάϊ τῆς Ἀθηνᾶς ἴδος ἐπιγραφὴν εἶχε τοιαύτην· Ἐγώ, εἰμι πᾶν τὸ γεγονὸς καὶ ὂν καὶ ἐσόμενον, καὶ τὸν ἐμὸν πέπλον οὐδείς πω θνητὸς ἀπεκάλυψεν.

[4] *Vid.* Tholuck, ibid. p. 193.

[5] So even yet, Wahrmund, Babylonierthum, Israelitenthum, Christenthum (1882), p. 119.

have the following testimony from Le Page Renouf:[1] "The words nuk pu nuk are indeed found in different passages of the Book of the Dead, and it is, moreover, true that nuk is the pronoun I, and that pu is often used as the relative pronoun to join the subject and predicate of a sentence. But we must examine the connection of the words before we may regard it as certain that we have before us a complete sentence, for pu generally stands at the end of a sentence. Now careful consideration of the passages in the Book of the Dead, where these words occur, shows us at once, that they teach us nothing, even divinely, regarding the essence of God. In one of these (lxxviii. 21) the deceased one says: 'I am he who knows the paths of nu;' in another (xxxi. 4): 'I am of old in the country (or in the fields)' . . . I am he, who is Osiris, of old, who confined his father Seb and his mother Nut on the day of the great carnage.'" In his other edition of the same Book of the Dead the words nuk pu nuk (chap. xcvi.) disappear, because the narrative is put in the third person. And accordingly it runs thus: "He the bull of the field, he is Osiris who confined his father," etc.

Or is Jahveh, the divine name, found to have been originally the possession of a Semitic tribe distinct from Israel? Now, no proof can be found to support the theory, put forward by von der Alm, Tiele, and Stade,[2]

[1] Le Page Renouf (in London), Lectures on the Origin and Development of Religion, explained by the religion of the ancient Egyptians (Autorisirte Uebersetzung, Leipzig 1881), p. 227 f.

[2] Richard von de Alm, ibid. pp. 216, 480; Tiele, Vergel. Gesch. 1872, p. 558 f.; Compendium, 1880, p. 94; Stade, Geschichte Israels, 1881, p. 130 f.

that Jahveh was originally the God of the Kenites, who were a tribe of the Midianites.¹ For, if we learn from 1 Chron. ii. 55 that the Kenites and the Rechabites were united, we read soon after in the clear narrative of 1 Chron. iv. 10 that the Kenite Jabez, now a settler in Judah, called on the God "of Israel." And as regards Jonadab the Rechabite (2 Kings x. 15 ff.), then dwelling amidst the ten tribes, it must be observed that he had preserved his ancestral faith, and thus differs from those of his countrymen who had adopted the worship of Jahveh. At least no other explanation has been given in explanation of his actions. And we may remember of the 7000 Israelites who remained faithful amidst prevalent defection (1 Kings xix. 18). Only the descendants of Jonadab must have preserved the faith in their adopted God of Israel (Jer. xxxv.). But it is highly improbable that the Kenites, who appear in a social and political view as strangers,—an element in the country allowed to exist, but having no say or interest in its government or institutions,—could have been the dominating element in moulding its religious history, from whom the Israelites had derived the most precious of all their possessions. They figure rather as strangers (Gerim) who have adopted the worship of Jahveh (Ex. xii. 48 ff.). And, do we not for the most part find that it is generally proselytes who are most zealous in the defence and upholding of their adopted faith? This surely cannot be counted strange, for they have adopted their new possession of their own will, while others have inherited it from their fathers,

---

[1] Ex. ii. 16; Judg. i. 16, iv. 11.

and, indeed, would require so to inherit it if they are to possess it at all.

Accordingly, thus differing from some modern scientists who regard the term יהוה as originating outside of Israel, and opposed as we are to the interpretation that it is only by the acceptance of this that the true spirit of critical reflection and historical impartiality is preserved, we are of the opinion that the historical consciousness of Israel itself should be laid upon the balance. For, according to its judgment, the Israelites have always recognised this divine name as their peculiar property; while, on the other hand, their traditions regard other religious phenomena as so many imports from strange lands. Tuch[1] has clearly shown us how this historical consciousness reveals itself in the Old Testament, making it plain even to the most casual observer that the Gentiles do not possess the true knowledge of Jahveh, but only the representation of the Deity in general terms. When used by them יהוה no longer signifies the true God, Creator of the universe, and Lord of the nations. On the other hand, it is limited to signify the God of the Hebrews, and was actually applied to idols (comp. 1 Kings xx. 23 with 28). With a distinct consciousness of all that is implied in the name יהוה, the true Hebrew in speaking to Gentiles does not use this term, preferring in its stead on such occasions the name אלהים. Accordingly, in Judg. i. 7, vii. 14, 1 Sam. iv. 7, 8, Jonah iii. 3 (with which compare v. 5, 8, 9, 10), and 1 Sam. xxx. 15, xxii. 3,[2] it is not to be regarded as uncommon

---

[1] Die Genesis erklärt (1838), p. xl. f.

[2] The apparent exceptions to this rule, as *e.g.* in 1 Sam. xxix. 6,

that אלהים is used with a plural construction, because by this the Jewish historian in his narrative takes up the standpoint of the heathen consciousness of God. And hence it is that the term יהוה is never used in any conversation carried on by the lower orders of creation (comp. *e.g.* Judg. ix. 9 with Gen. iii. 1 ff.).

The more recent supporters of von Bohlen's opinion (to whom we have already referred), which asserts that it was only after Moses' time that the term יהוה was adopted by Israel, differ from him, however, when he says that יהוה was borrowed from the Egyptians about the time of David or Solomon. They, on the other hand, imagine that this term was derived from the Canaanites [1] in their increased intimacy with Israel. The Mosaic origin of יהוה in its nature and surroundings has, however, been clearly demonstrated by Oort.[2] On this account it is sufficient for us to refer to Kuenen's [3] leading positions in his polemic directed against Land's treatise on the Canaanitish origin of the term יהוה. The first of these we meet with has reference to the

---

1 Kings x. 9, v. 21, 2 Kings xviii. 22, are explained by the fact that the narrative is more particularly concerned with its Jewish readers.

[1] *E.g.* Von der Alm, ibid. (1862) pp. 524-527 (comp. Dozy's German translation of his De Israelieten te Mecca, 1864, p. 39); Colenso, The Pentateuch, Part v. (1865), pp. 270 ff., with Land and Goldziher, of whom mention has already been made.

[2] De Dienst der Baalim onder Israel, § 17-51.

[3] De Godsdienst, i. pp. 397-401.

long-standing feud between the national God of Israel and the gods of Canaan. As Kuenen suggests, it is at the least improbable that the Deity which Israel served at the end of that struggle should be characterized by a Canaanitish name. But, secondly, Land is reminded that the names Jokabed, Joshua, and Jonathan (Moses' grandson) not merely reveal a knowledge of the name יהוה independent of Canaan, but, according to Deborah's Song (Judg. v. 4, 5), Jahveh, at war with the kings of Canaan, is spoken of as coming from Seir, from the region of Edom. And in connection with this Kuenen very properly places the question before Land: "Is it possible that Deborah, when she calls upon Jahveh as the 'God of Israel,' means that His origin was from Canaan, and not among themselves?" Thirdly, says Kuenen: "Land acknowledges that his view implies a turning aside from all Jewish tradition, for nowhere in the Old Testament do we find a single trace of the term Jahveh originating from Canaan." For these reasons, although not asserting that such an opinion should be altogether dismissed from our minds, yet, we must say, the reasons for receiving it must carry with them considerable weight. If Jahveh is the God of the Canaanites, let it be proved on clear and undeniable grounds. The testimony requisite for the support of this theory must be so arranged that it must be seen as something altogether apart from Jewish or even Old Testament influence. Although such proof may not be found from Macrobius, Saturnalia, i. 18, where Jao is spoken of as the chief among all gods, yet this reference, according to Diodorus Siculus, i. 94, has its origin from the later varieties of religion.[1] And now, lastly, we would draw the attention of our readers to the remark of Smend,[2] when he says: "The problem of the early conflict of Jewish idolatry is insoluble, if we do not accept the teaching, *e.g.*, of Deuteronomy, Ezekiel, and Lev. xvii. ff. (comp. also Num. xxv.; Hos. ix.) as faithful representations of fact. According to this, the national worship of more ancient Israel was, in great part at least, the worship of the gods of Canaan."[3] The religion of ancient Israel, however, uncondemned, did not trace its origin from Canaan.

[1] This has been already established by Tholuck, ibid. pp. 191-193, notwithstanding the reply which Land, in opposition to Kuenen's representations referred to above, published in the Theologisch Tijdschrift, 3 Bd. 1869, pp. 347-362. Graf Baudissin in his Studien zur semit. Religion, i. pp. 213-218, has according to our view rightly supported Kuenen's position. We have already remarked on the methodical worth which these words of Kuenen possess.

[2] Zeitschrift für die alttestl. Wissenschaft, ii. p. 107, Anm.

[3] Of Goldziher's hypothesis (Der Mythus bei den Hebräer, 1876, p. 327 ff.), in which he allows the adoption of the name Jahveh to have taken place since David's time, we shall speak under the seventh head of our inquiries.

Throughout these remarks, Kuenen, even in claiming a less developed character for the pre-prophetical Jahvism, has never asserted that the Tetragramm or its shorter form was originally in use among the Canaanites. Nay more, he does not for his own purposes rely upon the argument that the Israelites, in the name given to their God, have made use of the term Baal. But as this argument has been frequently used by men, foremost among those who advance and support these theories of development as a historical sign of the religious connection and being of the original Jahvism in Israel, we are compelled to refer to the fact of this questionable use of the word Baal, and to examine the teaching connected with it.

The question as to בעל being also used in the time of the Judges and early Kings to signify the revealed God is one which has been recently[1] answered in the affirmative by Herm. Schultz[2] and Dillmann.[3] With this opinion we agree. For at the outset we would remark the frequency with which the word Baal occurs in Hebrew (Ex. xxii. 28, etc.). And in

---

[1] In earlier times we have, *e.g.*, von Daumer, ibid. p. 109; Oort, De Dienst der Baalim, § 50, along with other Dutch writers; and von Wellhausen's Der Text der Bücher Samuelis (1871), pp. xii., 30, 31.

[2] Alttestamentliche Theologie, 1878, p. 482.

[3] Ueber Baal mit dem weiblichen Artikel (Monatsberichte der Academie der Wissenschaften zu Berlin, 16 June 1881), pp. 12-14.

addition to this we have the conjunct term Bealjah expressly mentioned (1 Chron. xii. 5). Then such *nomina propria*, compounded with Baal, have, for the most part, been used in those families which were specially zealous in upholding the national life and the national honouring of God (comp. Saul's son Eshbaal, 1 Chron. viii. 33, ix. 39; and David's son Beeliada, 1 Chron. xiv. 7). Finally, we find in Hosea (chap. ii. 16 f.) such an expression as the following: "And it shall be at that day, saith the Lord, that thou shalt call me Ishi; and shalt call me no more Baali. For I will take away the names of Baalim out of her mouth, and they shall no more be remembered by their name." Hosea is there prophesying that Israel is to designate Jahveh as Ish and no longer as Baal, signifying thereby the close union, as of a bride with her husband, subsisting between them as a people and Jahveh. And we are expressly informed by the prophet (ver. 16) that till then Jahveh had been called Baal by the people. In this respect the rendering of the term in the LXX. by Baaleim gives but uncertain assistance in the translation of this most difficult passage.[1] For, according to

---

[1] This is in opposition to Nestle, Die israelitischen Eigennamen, etc., p. 125.

this, the contents of ver. 16 cannot be said to correspond with those of the verse following. It would rather seem that the changed sign of Jahveh, predicted in ver. 16, appears as the consequence of the statement made in ver. 17: "I will take away the names of Baalim out of her mouth." This passage, however, is best explained in the recent works of Hitzig-Steiner [1] and Graf Baudissin.[2]

The main fact apparently to be gathered from this passage in Hosea is, that the *Nomen proprium* Baal was not used[3] in appealing to Jahveh, but rather as the *Nomen appellativum*.[4] This is clearly brought out in the suffix respectively found in Baali and Ishi. Viewed in this light the fact cannot be questioned, as Nowack[5] seeks to do, on the grounds that the sign of בעל, as applicable to Jahveh, seems scarcely comprehensible on account of the struggle against Baal-

---

[1] Die zwölf kleinen Propheten erklärt (a small exegetical handbook) 4th ed. 1881.

[2] *Vid.* the article "Baal" in the PRE², ii. p. 134.

[3] In the sense of *dominus maritus;* *e.g.* in the formula: O Lord; our Lord; my Covenant God or Consort.

[4] Hieronymus very clearly paraphrases the questionable words as follows: "Tantum odi, inquit Deus, idolorum nomina, ut etiam id, quod bene dici potest (*i.e.* that Jahveh as a Consort is called Baal, Gen. xx. 3, etc.), propter ambiguitatem et verbi similitudinem nequaquam velim dici." (Comp. Scholz, Commentar zum Buche des Propheten Hoseas, 1882.)

[5] Der Prophet Hosea erklärt (1880).

worship which took place in Ahab's time. But in the period preceding Elijah, according to Nowack, Jahveh, the Lord and Consort of Israel, was called Baal. This opinion, along with that expressed by Kuenen[1] and Nestle,[2] concerning the use of the term בעל as it appears in the proper names already mentioned (*e.g.* in the families of David and Saul), being a sign of the penetrating heathendom of the Canaanites, cannot be accepted as accurate.

According to the representation already recognised by us as to the former name of Jahveh being a form of Baal, we cannot imagine that pre-prophetic Israel had identified their God with the chief god of the Canaanites alike in nature, attributes, and the general relations to the world.

From the foregoing investigation the probable foundation is removed from the greater part of the proposition laid down by Tiele.[3] For, it has been already demonstrated that neither Saul nor David, in the names given to the members of their respective

---

[1] De Godsdienst, i. pp. 401–405.

[2] Die israelitischen Eigennamen, etc., p. 126.

[3] Compendium, p. 95 f.: "Even such zealous representatives of Jahvism as Saul and David called their children after Baal. Solomon, who built for Jahveh a magnificent temple, saw in this nothing to prevent him in erecting sanctuaries for other gods. This, no doubt, in the later writings, was regarded as sinful, but surely not by his con-

families, did use the expression Baal as a proper name, whether it be of the revealed God of Israel or the chief god of the Canaanites. But granted further, if it be not directly proved that Solomon's idol-worship, following as it did immediately after his zealous worship of God,[1] was not regarded against him for sin, nevertheless indirectly it had been shown throughout[2] that the religious traditions of the Jewish historical writings have not been amiss in that they were able to describe the appearance of Ahijah. This position is on all sides more safe than Tiele's broader hypothesis, that about Elijah's time the Phœnician Baal, which had been overcome, had given his own name to a so-called native Baal, and therefore, in Elijah's time, according to Tiele, the national Deity of Israel, already designated Jahveh, possessed two names, the one alongside of the other.[3]

temporaries. The Baal against whom Elijah so energetically struggled in the kingdom of Israel, was not the native, but the Phœnician god which the Zidonian princess Jezebel had introduced. His pupil Elisha and his follower Jehu successfully combined in their antagonism against this strange worship. They did not, however, interfere with the worship of the native Aschera."

[1] Chiefly as seen in the case of Ahijah at Shiloh, 1 Kings xi. 29-32.

[2] Comp. the inquiry followed out under Chap. III.

[3] We must call attention to the improbability of Tiele's view, that the expression Baal was at one time the name given to the God of Israel—a name no more existing in use or in the consciousness of the designation yet to be used by Israel.

Finally, from 1 Kings xvi. 31–33, the Aschera must be regarded in the same connection as the Phœnician Jezebel, joined as she was to the worship of Baal. Nor is the narrative concerned with an indigenous Aschera, for as it proceeds the "prophets of Baal" are alone spoken of (1 Kings xviii. 25, 40), and it is of this god that chief mention is made (1 Kings xix. 18; 2 Kings x. 18–29). According to 1 Kings xvi. 31, we are led to conclude that Baal, and not both, is spoken of as the masculine god, and in no way under any species of toleration are we justified in speaking of an indigenous goddess Aschera.

CHAPTER VI.

Was the idea of Jahveh in its full signification developed from the relation of the God of Israel to the other deities?—In the answer given to this question, on the part of those adhering to the development theories,[1] it has been regarded as a matter of secondary consideration. This, however, was in earlier times. Now it has been raised from this low position of secondary interest to one of chief importance.

The Development Theorists no doubt seem rightly to have represented the proposition [1] that in Israel the prophets and others of enlightened mind until just before Jeremiah's time, while still later the people themselves, had believed in the existence of other deities beside Jahveh. The following are the chief reasons by which we are led to make such a statement. The prophetic as well as the non-prophetic writings

---

[1] Till Kuenen. *Vid.* his Volksreligion und Weltreligion, pp. 316–319.

of the Old Testament (chiefly those of more ancient times) contain passages in which Jahveh not only is compared [1] with other gods, but is alone appropriated to Israel as a nation;[2] while the gods of the heathen are referred to as if they were realities.[3] Now, the comparison of Jahveh with other deities and His special appropriation in Israel do not in themselves afford sufficient proof that the existence of the Gentile gods was ever accepted by that portion of Israel faithful to Jahveh. Meanwhile, because the rebellious Israelites viewed the strange gods in the light of realities, and because it must have been given to the pious in Israel to recall the erring around them, and that not in any uncertain manner, we arrive at the explanation of the comparison of Jahveh with strange gods; the other facts already mentioned being used to show that the pious portion of Israel also believed in the reality of heathen deities. If, as Oehler[4] says, the intention of the faithless portion of Israel "was on all hands opposed as a perversion

---

[1] *E.g.* Micah vii. 18; Ex. xv. 11, xviii. 18; and to this list of passages we must add Deut. vi. 4, *i.e.* if we interpret it rightly (comp. Graf Baudissin, Studien, etc., i. p. 167).

[2] *E.g.* Micah iv. 5; Ex. xx. 2; Gen. ix. 26, xvii. 7 f.

[3] Isa. ii. 18, xix. 1, 3; Gen. xxviii. 19 f.; Judg. xi. 24; 1 Sam. xxvi. 19 f.; Ruth i. 15 ff., ii. 12.

[4] Theologie des A. T., § 43 (2nd ed. 1882, p. 155).

of the true idea of Jahveh imparted through the channels of revelation," we must say that this assertion in any unbiassed treatment of the Old Testament does not hold good.

But this knowledge, according to our understanding of the position assumed by the Development Theorists, has been obtained in an altogether wrong way. For as regards the unity and singular glory belonging to Jahveh, they would postulate the numerical as well as ideal monotheism existing in Israel as something not to be found in the religious consciousness of the people before Jeremiah's time. On the other hand, has it not often been asserted[1] that Jahveh was related to Israel as Kamos was to Moab, or, to interpret this comparison, what other does it mean than this, that we have in Jahveh and Kamos two great powers comparable the one with the other? This view, however, is not merely a direct contradiction given to the Jahveh worshipper when he says: "Who is a God like unto Thee?" or "Who is a God like unto Thee among the gods?"[2] but it goes against the general experience of Israel concerning their God. Regarding

---

[1] *E.g.* Kuenen, De Godsdienst, i. p. 222. Comp. also Stade, Geschichte Israels, pp. 4 f., 113-429.

[2] Micah vii. 18 ; Ex. xv. 11.

this de Wette's criticism of Vatke's work was certainly to the point. In that article he says:[1] "Development has succeeded according to Vatke's hypotheses; but in what a humble position he places Moses to whom he denies this consciousness,[2] while the latter, alike in his contact with the Egyptians and the other nations, and in the rich experience connected with the exodus from Egypt and the Wilderness journeys, not to mention traditional memories and earlier events, had recognised his God as the ruler of the universe." To this we must add the following circumstance, which is of decided weight in this formal crisis. The prophets contend not simply against a lower conception of God possessed by Israel in earlier times, when they describe Israel's God as the Creator of the universe and the Ruler of human history.[3]

Ghillany throughout his entire work on "Jahveh ist National Gott"[4] has again overlooked such a

---

[1] Theologische Studien und Kritiken, 1837, p. 998.

[2] *I.e.* of the immense superiority of God as revealed to him above all other strange gods.

[3] Amos iv. 12 f., v. 8, ix. 5, ii. 1, ix. 7; Zech. ix. 1; Micah iv. 13; Isa. x. 5, 15; comp. xxxvi. 10; Judg. v. 4, 5, but principally v. 20, where the stars are represented as fighting for Jahveh; Ex. xv. 7-10.

[4] Ibid. pp. 264-278.

passage as Amos ix. 7,[1] although he makes it a matter of boast [2] that he has not examined the Old Testament "through the orthodox spectacles, which can find nothing else in the Bible apart from the teaching of Paul." De Wette, however, has already brought forward, and justly so, what is to us a matter of first importance,[3] that the numerical monotheism which

---

[1] Stade repeats in the course of his History of Israel (1884, p. 429) the assertion that Jahveh was the God of Israel in the same degree as Chemosh was of Moab. In addition to this, however, he adds: "I cannot be regarded as differing from Amos ix. 7, where Jahveh is spoken of as leading the Syrians and the Philistines towards Canaan, for Amos held what might be called the development theory of God. This passage in Amos should be read from the standpoint of the old faith. So far at least as it speaks of Canaan." Risum teneatis, amici! (a) Are we to regard it as certain that Amos, differing altogether from his contemporaries, has ascribed to the God of Israel the government of the world? Does not even Stade himself (ibid. p. 358) say: "New ideas cannot be said to have been introduced to the religion of Israel through the older prophets"? (b) Does the new Hermath of the Syrians really belong to Canaan? Has not even Martin Schultze in his Handbook on Hebrew Mythology, p. 12, regarded Canaan as the Lowlands when compared with the "Highlands"?

[2] Ibid. p. 276.

[3] Biblische Dogmatik, 3rd ed. 1831, § 98: "Contrary to the suspicion that the Mosaic monotheism is nothing more than the privileged worship of the national God who existed along with other deities, the latter being, however, excluded from worship" (Lessing, Erziehung des Menschengeschlechts, §§ 11-15, 34, 35, and others), we hear the spiritual and moral voice speaking to us from the very nature of the Mosaic economy. Furthermore, the striking lack "of a mythology as well as of idol-worship, and lastly the clear monotheism of later Israel and their contempt for strange gods (e.g. Isa. ii. 11, xxvi.-xxviii.), are all against the suspicion alluded to."

we find in Israel in later times has for its hypothesis the ideal monotheism. Consequently, the right conclusion to be formed from such a basis is this, that the pre-prophetical religion of Israel contained the basis of true monotheism, which testified to the incomparable glory and most sublime power of the God of revelation. This view has been accepted by others, even by theologians belonging to the critical schools of more modern times. In connection with this, look, *e.g.*, at the statements of von Lengerke,[1] who has rightly asserted that from the consciousness, possessed by Israel, of the world-ruling position of their God, and according to the universal voice of prophecy, this question must be decided.[2] These voices, which regarded the God of Israel as the Creator, Preserver, Ruler, and Judge of the universe, and which proclaimed Him as the only object of worship for all nations in the future, had ere this been heard[3] (Isa. ii. 2–4 ; Micah iv. 1–3). And if the comparative novelty of this hope erected in the future is not once remarked on by the prophets, *i.e.*

---

[1] Kenaan (1844), pp. 484–486.

[2] In ibid. p. 494 : "The hope of seeing the Jahveh-worship extended to all the nations of the earth exhibits to us by reflection the tokens of a lofty religious consciousness of God." Comp. our more minute treatise on the Universality of the Religion of Israel.

[3] If not also already in Amos ix. 12.

Ancient Israel's Religion. 75

if this has not been regarded as the unfolding or development of an idea long cherished in Israel, that ought to be explained on reasonable grounds. For, from the view taken by Israel as to the world-position of her God, this universal hope for the future to which we have referred springs forth as a natural consequence. It is but the fruit which we might expect to find springing from such powerful seed. Or perhaps it were better for us to regard it in the light of its negative side. In this aspect of her future as seen in the judgment passed on her enemies[1] the direct positive separation is accomplished, and if this expectation is to be described in language, we gather from this merited destruction which comes upon the nation that only a part of the people would bow the knee before the Almighty God of Israel.[2]

As opposed to the correctness of the interpretation adopted on the part of theories of development, we have first of all the evidence adduced from the fact

[1] Amos i. 3, ii. 3. Already in this negative side the universality of prophecy is to be found.

[2] Ewald (Lehre der Bibel von Gott, i. p. 106) has also rightly decided that Moses even had comprehended in a perfect degree the unity and spirituality of God, and Hitzig has justly said (Vorlesungen über Bibl. Theologie, etc., § 8): "Before Jahveh the idolatrous nations were dispersed." The same standpoint is taken up by Herm. Schultz (Alttestl. Theologie, p. 447 ff.) and Nestle (Die israelitischen Eigennamen, etc., pp. 142-145). Comp. also Reuss, Geschichte des A. T.

that they can in no way prove as groundless the old view, according to which the ideal monotheism was inseparably connected with the recognised superiority of Jahveh. And, in addition to this, there is the weighty circumstance that from their standpoint they are unable to prove a trustworthy source from which they can trace the transformation by which the national God Jahveh has passed into the God of the world. Kuenen has exercised his mind with this question, as we see from p. 118 of his latest work.

First of all, he imagines that as the idea of God in Israel was associated with that of supreme power, it resembled the ideas about God prevalent among other nations. For the Moabite has always regarded his Chemosh, and the Ammonite his Malkhâm, as more powerful than the gods of other nations. Granted in the meantime that the Moabites had compared their god with Jahveh, we must first of all show that they

§ 269, and paragraph 11 of Graf Baudissin's article reviewing Kuenen's Volksreligion und Weltreligion in the Theolog. Literaturzeitung, 1883, p. 318. In this review he says: "We lay as much emphasis as formerly on the understanding of prophecy, that already the older prophets were monotheists. They, however, did not in themselves possess the knowledge that Jahveh for the present was the only Deity for the heathen." Kautzsch explains his position in the Theolog. Literaturzeitung of 29th Dec. 1883, col. 603, justly objecting to the crude interpretation of the Jewish idea of God of the tenth and eighth centuries.

regarded their god as incomparable, relegating to him the position of the world's ruler and the guide of its history. In this respect Kuenen has erred in that he views pre-prophetic Israel as ascribing the idea of might alone to their God, while they, on the other hand, had to a much greater extent realized in their God the boundless capacity of a real and verbal mani-festation. And, consequently, it is of Him as viewed in this light that they speak.

Equally at fault is Kuenen's position when he accepts the view—imaginary and untenable as it is—that Jahveh, born out of the national feeling, and with its growth become proportionately powerful, had equally suffered under the disasters which had destroyed the national consciousness; yea more, that He must become weak and at last pass away among the perishing memories of a sinking race. Now, we may well ask, what answer do the facts of history give to this view as put forward by the Development Theorists? It is simply this, that if Israel had regarded the power of their God to be inseparable from the history of the post-Mosaic period, or if Israel had not obtained under Moses and Joshua a lasting impression of the unique grandeur of his supernatural Being, connected as that was with all history, it follows that faith in Jahveh had disappeared from Israel long before the time of the writing prophets.

To his idea of the monotheism as possessed by the prophets, Kuenen adds further that the pre-prophetical God of Israel may be said to possess feelings in common with the other deities, while, on the other hand, the moral attributes which the people have generally ascribed to Jahveh were in a peculiar measure the means, though not essentially so, by which He was separated from His rivals. Meanwhile we must here ask if holiness in its moral significance had not ere this been ascribed to God by pre-prophetical Israel? For let it be kept in view, although the pretended development of the Old Testament idea of holiness is not at present before us, that it was in the name of this God that the priests spoke rightly; it was by His representatives that the tribes of Israel, unmindful of duty, were found fault with and cursed;[1] and, finally, it was by His messenger Nathan that David, the king of Israel, was rescued from his erring ways to the paths of rectitude.[2]

Lastly, we thus see that the ground of the new foundation which Kuenen has endeavoured to create for the prophetical monotheism has been removed.

[1] Judg. v. 15-18, 23.   [2] 2 Sam. xii. 1-10.

He imagines, *e.g.*, that in the consciousness of the prophets it is no longer the power but the holiness of Jahveh which occupies the central position; and in addition to this, he informs us that the idea of God has been transposed into another and higher sphere, and thereby it is that Jahveh was placed in a position of such decided contrast to the other deities.¹ First of all, however, we may remark it is not the case that by the writing prophets the holiness of Jahveh had been viewed in an altogether different way than by the earlier worshippers of Jahveh,² as if they had given it an altogether different place among the divine attributes. Such a proposition, from which Kuenen wished to derive these two phenomena of fundamental import, viz. the possibility of contrast between the true and false prophets,³ and the monotheism of the Old Testament appearing at a comparatively late period in the national history, and characterized by distinct phases of development as if it had originated in merely human representations,—such a proposition, we say, is entirely deprived of any historical basis.

---

¹ Kuenen (ibid.): "If Jahveh be God, the Holy One, they cannot be regarded in the same light. In one word, from the ethical idea of ahveh's essence must we trace the origin of this unity."

² Regarding this we have somewhat more to say farther on.

³ Comp. my Offenbarungsbegriff des A. T., i. p. 35.

For not only have we shown in the preceding section how at all times Israel has ascribed holiness to Jahveh, but at the same time as a people they possessed a clear consciousness of human frailty and sin. Not only have Amos and Hosea denounced the sins of their nation, but they have portrayed with graphic clearness the coming judgment by Jahveh. In this they are not alone, for their work but resembles that of Isaiah, who speaks of Jahveh as "the Holy One of Israel." And not only these, but to them we may add in no less degree the names of Micah, Nahum, Jeremiah, and the other prophets, although it may be that they do not use with Isaiah such a phrase as "the Holy One of Israel;" nay, even if they do not regard the holiness of Jahveh as the principal theme in their message to men. In that case this idea of Jahveh's holiness, the central of those attributes accorded to Him by the writing prophets, does not afford us that proof which we might expect from it. For how little explanation has been given as to how the true prophets could be convinced[1] of the justice of those threats of judgment sent forth by them! So far, however, as this is concerned, we must take our stand by the side

---

[1] In opposition to Kuenen we have already proved this. Comp. our Offenbarungsbegriff des A. T., i. p. 35.

of the old representation of the facts. By this we see that the true prophets for long, and even in Isaiah's time, were one and all convinced of the truth of their message by the source from which that message came. We might also say in this respect that the rise of monotheism in Israel has been as little explained, because mention of the numerical (*i.e.* the definite) monotheism is not connected with the holiness of Jahveh, but first appears in Jeremiah.

The so-called "ethical monotheism of the prophets" is also a vain invention of the Development Theorists. The idea is that the position reached in the experiences of Moses' time, viz. the conviction of the unique grandeur of the God of Israel, has produced its own consequences parallel to the progressive manifestation —real and verbal as that has been—of the revealed God. In other words, the view now long positively expressed as to the unique grandeur of Jahveh has at last found its negative formula when contrasted with the idols of the great power of Further Asia which overthrew the people of Jahveh. On the one hand, neither has the sign of holiness been wanting in the pre-prophetical conception of Jahveh, nor on the other is the idea of omnipotence amiss in the idea of God as it is held by the writing prophets. Omnipotence and holiness have not changed, and need not be changed, in the framing of the true idea of God, in that they describe two different yet equally necessary aspects of the divine nature. The idea of God as possessed by Israel was not placed by the writing prophets in another higher sphere, and by these same prophets it cannot be said that the holiness of Jahveh was first spoken of in contrast to the other deities. Long ere Isaiah had proclaimed Jahveh as "the Holy One of Israel," Amos (iii. 7) had realized that the causal nexus of the world's history had its deepest roots in the real and verbal self-manifestation of the God of Israel. And, equally with Amos, the 7000 followers of Jahveh have possessed the same experience, for, emulating the zealous Elijah, they had not bowed the knee before Baal (1 Kings xix. 18). And not only by Elijah; we find the same truth to have been equally realized by Samuel as he raised his Eben-ezer,—a monument to the actual power of God as witnessed in history, — with its inscription, "Hitherto hath the Lord helped me" (1 Sam. vii. 12). These men could not have gained such a knowledge at the time of the political overthrow of Jahveh's people, but must have inherited it from Moses, as the universal tradition of Israel affirms.

For it was Moses who, as the hand of God, dispersed the enemies of Israel on every hand, and affirmed it as his experience that Jahveh, and He alone among all those regarded as deities, deserved the name of God (Ex. xv. 6, 11).[1]

Without looking further into the minutiæ of the question with which we have been dealing, we would ask if traces can now be found of a religion of Baal or Moloch which occupied the same high level with the worship of Jahveh, engaged in as that was by those who remained faithful to the tradition of their fathers? While the supporters of the Development theory assume the answer to such a question to be in the affirmative, they none the less recognise the apparent yet comprehensible superiority which the worship of

---

[1] Goldziher (Der Mythus bei den Hebräern (1876), p. 327 ff.) has imagined that it was in the political and religious centralization carried on under David that the phenomenon began, which Goldziher calls "the working out of the monotheism as found in Elohim," and which in its various grades has maintained its distinct expression in the form ha-elohim = ὁ Θεός. Because the Canaanites have used this term Elohim, it is concluded that the *Nomen proprium* Jahveh has been formulated since David's time. But, on the other hand, Nestle, Die israelitischen Eigennamen (1875), p. 138, has rightly inquired: "If elohim or ha-elohim had been necessary as the sign of God, does the need still exist of creating a proper name for Him? Has not much more come out of Jahveh, the God of Israel, the God κατ' ἐξοχήν, than from ha-elohim, or, lastly, of Elohim alone? And where is proof to be found that the Israelites had ever used ha-elohim or Elohim as a proper name?"

that supernatural Being possessed for the real follower of Jewish tradition. For was it not He who, at the critical periods of Israel's history, had vouchsafed grace and strength to the people, and had established for Himself strong claims to their gratitude and esteem?

CHAPTER VII.

Was there a development of Jahvism in the representation of Jahveh's character?— It is with reference to the substance of Jahveh that we witness the progress accomplished in the Jewish representations. Here Israel has distinctly risen from the grade of a natural religion to a position, as men regard it, of the first truly spiritual and worthy idea of God. The progress has been from the idea of Jahveh as a fire to the representation of Jahveh as of an abstraction —a form of spiritual existence. So said not only Daumer,[1] but Ghillany,[2] "Jahveh is fire;" while Ernest Meier[3] speaks of Him as "the light-giving Heaven." And Kuenen,[4] going further, regards such comparisons of Jahveh with light or fire as sufficient

---
[1] Der Feuer- und Moloch-dienst, pp. 18-22.
[2] Die Menschenopfer, pp. 278-298.
[3] Tübinger Theol. Jahrb. i. (1842), p. 473; comp. also K. Plank, vol. iv. (1845), p. 478.
[4] De Godsdienst, i. p. 240.

grounds to be found even in the prophetical utterances[1] for establishing the original relationship subsisting between Jahveh and Moloch. On the other hand, however, it did not appear to Kuenen that God, as viewed by the later Israel, did not possess a real existence, but existed in their minds as an idea of philosophy, while the Spirit of God was regarded as an abstraction.[2]

According to our view of the matter, neither of the two points alluded to—the supposed commencement as well as the conclusion of the questionable development—is to be derived from the Old Testament.

1. Proof which gainsays the assertion that, by the pre-prophetical Jahvism, the essence of God was regarded as fire.

Even according to Kuenen himself, Jahveh is only compared to fire and light by the prophets. And he

---

[1] Amos v. 6; Isa. x. 17, xxx. 27, xxxii. 14, comp. also iv. 5, xxx. 30, 33, xxxi. 9.

[2] *Vid.* Kuenen's Volksreligion und Weltreligion, p. 124: "That which unveiled itself before the spiritual eye of the prophets was nothing less than the idea of a moral government of the universe. Into the changeable connection between nature's strength and workings the prophets have no insight. They do not think of the possibility of looking back for a reason, or even leading up to one. But they saw clearly, so far back as their vision extended, the realization of a plan which revealed to them not simply the tumult of the nations, but also collected nature made serviceable in the working out of a preconceived aim."

is obliged to confess,[1] "We are not liable to mistake that the pious men in Israel, because they used such expressions,[2] appeared to speak in metaphors. For them Jahveh had long ceased to be one of the many gods of nature; He is in their estimation the only true God" (2 Sam. xxii. 32). The Old Testament view, however, if we look carefully into it, we shall find as follows. In reality lightning was only the form by which God revealed Himself. It is so, for example, when as a smoking furnace and flame of fire the Godhead passed through the parts of the sacrifice prepared by Abraham (Gen. xv. 17); when the thornbush burned but was never consumed (Ex. iii. 2); when the cloud and pillar of fire conducted Israel through the desert (Ex. xiii. 21); when the fiery chariot and horses bore Elijah heavenwards (2 Kings ii. 11), and afterwards were round about Elisha (2 Kings vi. 17); and when from the throne of God fire unfolded itself (Ezek. i. 4). Therefore, reproducing the prophetical experiences, the Psalmist sings: "Thou coverest Thyself with light as with a garment" (Ps. civ. 2). In the New Testament we find it written:

---

[1] De Godsdienst, i. p. 240.
[2] Ex. iii. 2, xxiv. 17; Deut. iv. 24; comp. also ix. 3; 2 Sam. xxii. 9.

"The glory of the Lord shone round about them" (Luke ii. 9); and the face of Christ at the Transfiguration, when His inner realm of light broke through but for a moment, shone like the sun (Matt. xvii. 2). In addition to these, compare the δόξα disclosed to our Lord at the time of sore distress (John xii. 28, xvii. 5); and light spoken of as the dwelling-place of the Divine Spirit (1 Tim. vi. 16). "God dwells in the light which no man can approach unto."

Now, on what grounds can it be proved that the secret essence of Jahveh was in the olden time identified by His true followers with fire or light? From the traces which, in Kuenen's opinion, show the relationship which the ancient Jahveh-worship had with that of Moloch? These imaginary traces are the human sacrifices or their weaker equivalents which were offered to the Old Testament Jahveh, in whose sight they were well-pleasing. Regarding this, however, we hope to speak further on when we treat of the questionable development of the Old Testament conception of Jahveh's holiness. In any case, from such sources we can only judge of the character of Jahveh, apart altogether from His essence.

Or, that they may prove fire and light as the transcendental nature of God, do they wish to refer to the necessary or probable[1] connection existing between Jahveh and the heavenly deities of the Semites? With regard to this, however, even on the basis of comparative religious science, an exact exegesis is opposed to such a supposition. In contrast to this theory, we find that Israel's God from the beginning had possessed this celestial character as a branch of the widely-spread Ssabäismus. Indeed, the term Ssebaoth as applied to Jahveh in reality first appears in Samuel's time, and had formerly no reference to the stars. This expression, moreover, of which we have been speaking, cannot be regarded as an ancient name for God, nor even in the light of an element in patriarchal or Mosaic religion.[2]

[1] *E.g.* Pfleiderer, ibid. p. 357: "The near relationship between Jahveh and the light and fire divinities of the Semites is made more than probable, in that the traces of His nature have not been altogether lost sight of in the spiritual comprehensions of the prophets. And we may rightly conclude that such traces, which not only suit the spiritual aspect of Jahvism, and accordingly the more resemble some mental imagery, must originally have had some special signification attached to them in that they set forth what had yet to be understood of the divine essence."

[2] With regard to the uncertainty of the religious tradition of Israel, if we cannot on the one hand agree with Daumer, yet on the other we may accept with Tiele as certain a fixed and definite essence of tradition. In doing so, however, we cannot speak with him (Compendium, p. 97) of "a purely national worship of sun, moon, and stars, which not a few in Israel faithfully observed even in the time of the writing prophets." The Old Testament position is adhered to by Schrader in his article "Sterne" in Schenkel's Bibellexicon, v. p. 395, as well as by Riehm in his Handwörterbuch des Bibl. Alterthums, p. 1551.

What signification, we may now ask, has the Old Testament attached to the late Jewish consciousness, and to the term applied to God in Samuel's time? (*a*) According to the authentic explanations of Scripture itself,[1] we find Ssebaoth applied to the earthly hosts of Israel urged into conflict on behalf of Jahveh. The name is the outcome of the warlike glory of Israel which had begun with Samuel:—*e.g.* compare the explanation of "Jahveh Ssebaoth" as applied to the "God of the armies of Israel," 1 Sam. xvii. 45; the description of Jahveh as "the God of Battle," Ps. xxiv. 8, Isa. xiii. 4; and also the general language of Ps. xliv. 9, "Thou goest not forth with our armies." In such instances Jahveh is represented as the leader of the Jewish host, and on this account the enemy was regarded as already overcome (2 Sam. v. 24). The use of the term has been so regarded by Herder,[2] von Cölln,[3] Gustav Baur,[4] Herm. Schultz, Alttest. Theologie, p. 492; Schrader, article "Ssebaoth" in Schenkel's Bibellexicon

---

[1] Ex. vii. 4, xii. 41, 51.

[2] Werke zur Religion und Theologie. Stuttgart 1827-30. Vol. ii. p. 166. *E.g.*, "David first used the name 'The Lord of hosts' against the Philistines (1 Sam. xvii. 45), and proclaims it as the name of God who orders Israel's battles, *i.e.* as one who fights on their behalf."

[3] Biblische Theologie, 1836, p. 104.

[4] *Vid.* the 5th ed. of de Wette's Commentary on the Psalms, 1856, p. 171.

(1875), and in the Jahrbücher für protestantische Theologie, i. (1875) pp. 316 ff.; and finally, Grätz, Geschichte der Juden, i. p. 259. (β) All these learned men have decided that in later times[1] "Jahveh Ssebaoth" was used not only in leading the armies of Israel, but the term Ssebaoth signified the union of the earthly armies with the stars and angels. "The early thoughtful but limited idea," says von Cölln (ibid. p. 105), "was, with the prophets, alike spiritual and comprehensive, resembling the idea of a universal ruler ($\pi\alpha\nu\tau o\kappa\rho\acute{a}\tau\omega\rho$), a term already appropriated in the LXX. for Ssebaoth." Graf Baudissin has also accepted a more original and more modern idea of the expression Jahveh Ssebaoth (Studien zur Semit. Religionsgeschichte, i. 1876, pp. 119-123). (γ) On the other hand, however, we must remember, in addition to the circumstances already mentioned, that the term Ssebaoth was not, up to this point, found in Hebrew literature, it being simply used with reference to the armies of Israel. Hitherto Ssebaoth signified the hosts of stars and angels,[2] and we find

---

[1] *E.g.* Amos, Hosea (xii. 6), Isaiah, Micah, Nahum, Habak., Zeph., Jer., Hag., Zech., Mal.

[2] *Vid.* Delitzsch, Zeitschrift für die gesammte Lutherische Theologie und Kirche, 1874, pp. 217-222. Fr. W. Schultz in Zöckler's Handbuch der Theol. Wissenschaften, i. p. 299.

that God's heavenly host always appears in the singular form (Sseba' haschschamajim). This expression signifies the stars (Deut. iv. 19, xvii. 3; 2 Kings xvii. 16) and angels (1 Kings xxii. 19; 2 Chron. xviii. 18; Neh. ix. 6; Gen. xxxii. 2; Josh. v. 13; Isa. xlv. 12). This singular form is also used by the Psalmist (cxlviii. 2) in his use of צְבָאוֹ. No doubt this has been accepted in the punctuation of the text, but it was evidently not understood that it should be pronounced as ssebaav. This pronunciation was both unnecessary and wrong, in that no plural form ssebaim exists. Even from the solitary instance of צְבָאָיו, found in Ps. ciii. 21, we cannot conclude that this plural form existed as a living form in the language. The ending av is more frequently than otherwise written in the singular form with God. (For examples of this see my Historisch-Kritisch Lehrgebäude der Hebr. Sprache, i. 1881, p. 49.)

Lastly, however, can it be said that the Old Testament itself affords traces that the expression Jahveh originally contains a moral idea of greatness, as the meaning from the first attached to it? In answer to this, we would point to Gen. xix. 24, "And the Lord rained upon Sodom and upon Gomorrah brimstone and fire from Jahveh out of heaven;" and Micah v. 7, where it is written, "As a dew from Jahveh." In addition to this, however, does the term יהוה appear to have been used for " heaven " ?

The so-called traces of this have been carefully shown by Ewald[1] in his endeavour to find out the satisfactory significance of the Tetragramm in contrast to Ex. iii. 14; further, by J. G. Müller[2] in his aim to found upon them the relationship subsisting between the Hebrew idea of God and the Indo-Germanic Jews or Jupiter; and still more by Hitzig,[3] partly for the same reason, partly because the Hebrews in later times spoke of " heaven " as being equivalent to God, and partly because the heathen reproached Judah for honouring heaven. All these, however, are *per se* not trustworthy arguments. Accordingly Herm. Schultz[4] has already spoken of Ewald's position as extremely doubtful. We can, however, agree with Dillmann[5] when he speaks of the phrase " from the side of Jahveh " as being synonymous with the expression " out of heaven." According to the teaching of the Old Testament, where Israel's God[6] is always represented as a

---

[1] Geschichte des Volkes Israels, ii. p. 223.
[2] Die Semiten, etc. (1872), p. 163.
[3] Vorlesungen über Bibl. Theol., etc., § 7, 1.
[4] Theologie des A. T., p. 487.
[5] Die Genesis erklärt (1882).
[6] As Hitzig has rightly acknowledged in his Vorlesungen über Bibl. Theologie, § 7, 2.

person, יהוֹ has attached to it the meaning it possesses in Micah, "Dew from Jahveh," and signifies "the possessor of heaven,"— the Most High God whose priest Melchisedek was (Gen. xiv. 19).

We may therefore conclude that no proof is to be derived from the Old Testament, where the essence of the revealed God of Israel might be represented as signifying the ordinary idea of greatness.

2. Proof which opposes and contradicts the assertion that Jahveh as worshipped by the prophets was a mere abstraction.

We affirm that the God of the prophets was no imaginary being, no mere idea, but something real, something definite, although no part of Him may be visible. First of all, God as set forth by the prophets has been represented as pure Spirit, so far as His essence is concerned. Accordingly Oehler[1] is right when he says: "In the prophecies of the Old Testament the Spirit is always spoken of as God's life or element" (comp. Isa. xl. 13; Ps. cxxxix. 7; and for a contrast to this, Isa. xxxi. 3). "There the rûach or spirit corresponds to êl." Lengerke[2] also ascribes an immaterial being to God as revealed in the Old

---

[1] Alttest. Theologie, § 46.   [2] Kenaan, p. 482.

Testament. Hitzig[1] even acknowledges that "God was regarded as a Spirit," and most suitably draws attention to 1 Kings xix. 13, where a still soft voice is the accompanying covering, if not quite the element of God, as He appeared to Elijah. In addition to these we have Herm. Schultz, who is afraid of conceiving by the senses what is in reality above conception.[2] He says: "God as a Spirit is not the theme of prophecy. It is the Spirit of God which we meet with.[3] In the representation of Isa. xxxi. 3 we find what may be generally regarded as the teaching of the Old Testament." Lastly, Ewald[4] has openly given it as his opinion: "As Christ so well presented the truth in such a short sentence (John iv. 24), it had previously been so depicted by Moses. This we might say was accomplished in the revelation granted through Moses, and forms the only groundwork of all relationship between God and man."

The expression "Spirit of God," which we meet with in the Old Testament, has been already defended and supported in opposition to recent assertions such as made by Kuenen (comp. my Offenbarungsbegriff

[1] Vorlesungen über Bibl. Theologie, p. 50.
[2] Alttest. Theologie, p. 467.
[3] Ibid. p. 469.
[4] Lehre der Bibel von Gott., ii. p. 125.

des A. T., i. pp. 126-133). The Spirit is regarded throughout the Old Testament as having a real existence, and is everywhere represented as exercising supernatural power.

As this spiritual substance thus collected forms the only real, and is alone preserved from change and dissolution, so is it the God of Israel—the origin of life for the universe—the unity of all collected things.[1] For it is not only in the historical revelation that we see the glory of God manifested on every hand, but it is seen in the future depicted to His people. In that realm of glory God shall exceed the brightness of the sun and moon (Isa. lx. 19). Thus the substance of God may be regarded as something which sparkles or shines forth at every move.

[1] Isa. xxxvii. 4, 17; Jer. x. 10; Num. xiv. 21, 28; Ps. xlii. 3.

CHAPTER VIII.

Do we find in Jahvism any development with respect to the image of Jahveh?—Have the true worshippers at any time recognised as true the representation of Jahveh in the form of an image, so that there was no religious mistake committed by them in the setting up of such images, no denial or setting aside of the Jewish conception of God?[1] This is the decisive question for us to answer in the inquiry to which we have at present set ourselves.

We find that certain domestic animals[2] were used in representation of Jahveh, not only in their wilderness journey, but also in the kingdom of the ten tribes (Ex. xxxii. 8, 23 ; 1 Kings xii. 28). Regarding their

---

[1] In opposition to the assertions of Daumer (ibid. p. 117) and Ghillany (ibid. pp. 289-358), Lengerke (ibid. pp. 482-84) and Noack (Mythologie und Offenbarung, p. 297) have already defended this on the basis of Old Testament criticism.

[2] עגל has not the signification of "Ass," as Daumer makes out, for the meanings affixed to the names of animals frequently change. Moreover, accepting this meaning, the old supposition of the Jews

origin there are essentially three sources to which we are referred, all of which have found more or less support. First of all, we might say that the bull as an image of the Deity was borrowed from the worship of strange nations. Or, secondly, it arose out of the patriarchal worship of the Hebrews, and was popular, though always an inheritance endured but mourned over. In this sense it was a renewal of the old experiences of Israel. Or, thirdly, the worship of the bull may be the legally Mosaic as well as post-Mosaic way of worshipping Jahveh.

Although the Old Testament does not directly speak of an Egyptian origin of the representation of Jahveh by an animal, yet this origin is pointed out in an indirect manner. For not only do we find the image of the animal instituted by the people shortly after their exodus from Egypt, but it was renewed at a later period by Jeroboam I., who himself had sojourned in Egypt. In addition to this, even according to the consciousness of the people as that is revealed in

---

worshipping the ass is explained (Joseph. c. Ap. 2. 7, comp. Tacit. Hist. 5. 3). Only the ass is mentioned as an unclean animal (Ex. xiii. 13); and the impurity of animals coincides with their historical position (see Robertson Smith, "Animal Worship," etc., in Journal of Philology, vol. ix. (1880) p. 97). There the word עגל is reckoned along with its feminine as cattle, and can have had no other signification as object of worship.

Ezekiel, we find it was during their residence that they had polluted themselves with the Egyptian idols (Ezek. xx. 7, 8; Josh. xxiv. 14), and had brought with them from Egypt their idolatry (Ezek. xxiii. 3, 8, 19, 21); while after their settlement in Canaan we are told that they lent themselves to the unbelief " of the Egyptians their neighbours" (Ezek. xvi. 26, with which comp. viii. 7–13). Now all this goes to prove that in idolatrous practices Israel followed the example set them by their Egyptian neighbours, which idolatry Ezekiel regards as existing in Israel prior to their oppression by the Philistines (xvi. 27). The prophet, however, may have mentioned the thraldom of the Philistines instead of that of Babylon, it being the heaviest which Israel had to endure (1 Sam. xiii. 19–23). This circumstance, however, in no way gainsays the fact that Israel in Ezekiel's time was aware of the Egyptian idolatry which had been practised in Canaan. In reality, the representation of Jahveh by means of an animal has been regarded by not a few scientists of more recent times as an imitation of the worship of Apis and Mnevis.[1]

[1] *E.g.* von Kurtz, Geschichte des alten Bundes, ii. (1858) p. 314; Keil, Archäologie, 2nd ed. 1875, § 90; Delitzsch in Riehm's Handwörterbuch des Bibl. Alterthums, p. 1116; de Wette, Archäologie, 3rd ed. (1842) § 193; von Lengerke, Kenaan, p. 553; Thenius on 1 Kings

In our opinion, the origin of the bull-image, which has been so much discussed on every hand, is by no means incapable of explanation. For, although living animals were the objects of the Egyptian worship, and even in their priestly processions and in the temples there are images of sacred animals to be found, yet the decision which satisfies Le Page Renouf [1] even less

xii. 28; J. G. Müller, Die Semiten, p. 152; Ewald, Die Alterthümer des Volkes Israels, 3rd ed. p. 299; Hitzig, Vorlesungen über Bibl. Theologie, p. 26; Keinert in his article on Jeroboam, in Riehm's Handwörterbuch; Grätz, Geschichte der Juden, i. p. 44. Besides these, the term אָבִיר (hero, Gen. xlix. 24; Isa. i. 24) has been taken from the Egyptian Apis, because אַבִּיר (strong, Ps. xxii. 13; Isa. xxxiv. 7) in refined language signified an animal. This has been already stated by von Lengerke (Kenaan, p. 464), and is no new discovery made by Grätz (ibid. p. 370). But the assertion is also incorrect— 1st, Because "abbir" generally signifies "strong," and also has been used to denote the prince (Ps. lxviii. 31). 2nd, Because as it signifies the animal, so it also does the horse (Jer. viii. 16, xlvii. 3, l. 11). 3rd, Because it is not expressly called Apis (Jer. xlvi. 15). *Abir* cannot be regarded as a sure sign of Egyptian influence on Jewish thought. Such a term rather reminds us of the strong eagle which on his mighty pinions bore Israel from Egypt unto himself (Ex. xix. 4, xxxii. 11; Ps. xci. 4).

[1] Vorlesungen über die Religion der alten Aegypter (Leipzig 1881), p. 288: "To trace back the superstition or idolatry of the Israelites to an Egyptian source seems to us quite unreasonable. Men wish to recognise in the golden calf a representation of Apis or Mnevis; but for such an assumption there is not sufficient proof at our disposal. The worship of bulls as symbols of the Deity was not peculiar to the Egyptians; it is to be found in all religions. The chariot and horses of the sun, which the kings of Judah had placed at the entrance of the temple, and which Joas [!] destroyed with fire, are sufficient proof in themselves that Israel as a nation possessed its own mythology." [!]

than others reveals at the best but a superficial regard for the Old Testament. In Goshen or its boundaries[1] was situated the town On, in which the bright-coloured bull (Mnevis) was worshipped. Although it happened that the calf was made in the wilderness to represent the God of Israel, that God who had proved Himself so mighty against Egypt, it none the less seems to us that too much stress has been laid on this circumstance. A meaning, in fact, has been brought out of it which it cannot be said to possess. For the question is not as to how Israel, newly delivered from Egypt, could worship an Egyptian god; but it is concerned with the possibility of Israel choosing an Egyptian image as the visible form of their God. The question put in this way appears incapable of being negatived in an absolute form. Israel not only looked back with desire upon the fish and vegetables of Egypt (Num. xi. 5), but we can trace the Egyptian influence on the ancient worship of Israel. As an example of this, we have but to remember the origin of the Urim and Thummim, which in all probability has come from Egypt.

In answering this question thus set before us, no special weight can be laid on the fact mentioned in

[1] Comp. Ebers in Riehm's Handwörterbuch des Bibl. Alterthums, p. 1111.

2 Chron. xi. 15, that Jeroboam I. had ordained priests to the Seirim. For since the signification attached to these idols is not explained, and because in Isa. xiii. 21 and xxxiv. 14 they are used in no relation whatever to Egypt, the forbidden impurity referred to in Lev. xvii. 7, xviii. 23, xx. 15, 16, cannot be traced back to the goat-worship of Egypt. With this last-mentioned probability it is impossible for us to agree, because the goat is not mentioned by them; because this impurity is forbidden to men as well as to women; and lastly, because the abominations of the Canaanites are even more emphasized than those of Egypt (Lev. xviii. 3, xx. 22).[1]

We are more inclined to the belief that the representation of Jahveh by an animal was borrowed from the Egyptians. This seems more probable, and more in accordance with a correct interpretation of the Old Testament than those views put forward in recent times by certain critics. If the image of the bull could be an image of the worship of the Canaanites, we may with certainty conclude that many elements of Israel's backslidings can be traced to Canaanitish

---

[1] Von Bohlen has already remarked (Genesis, 1835, p. clxxvi.): "Ezekiel complains of all these vices" (xxii. 10, 11), etc. Smend's remark is also to the point. (*Vid.* Die Genesis des Judenthums, ibid. p. 140.)

influence.[1] This image of the bull cannot, however, be traced to such a source. It is nowhere, on the other hand, associated with the Moloch of the Ammonites, while the religious influence exercised by the Assyrians, according to the testimony of the Old Testament, began at a comparatively late period in Israel's history.

On the other hand, however, the newly-approved representation of Jahveh as a bull traced to an old Jewish origin, presents difficulties of no mean sort.[2] For at the outset one must ask how no trace of such idol-worship is to be found in the history of Abraham. And we cannot suppose, from the original data at our disposal, that tradition had endeavoured to purify the heroes of the past, freeing them so far as possible from all connection with religious or moral backsliding. No doubt we are told of idols being in Jacob's family (Gen. xxxi. 19), but nowhere is the image of the bull mentioned. As to this, Herm. Schultz (ibid. p. 101) says that the image of the calf in the wilder-

---

[1] Ezek. xvi. 3, 15-25; Deut. xii. 2; 1 Kings xi. 1.

[2] Herm. Schultz, Alttestl. Theologie, p. 101; Dillmann in his Commentary on Exodus and Leviticus at Ex. xxxii. 4; Diestel in his article "Goldenes Kalb," in Riehm's Handwörterbuch, p. 807; Graf Baudissin in his article on the same subject in the Protestant Realencyclopädie, vii. (1880) p. 395; Kautzsch in his article "Jeroboam," vi. (1880) p. 637; Oehler, Alttestl. Theologie, § 172.

ness, associated as it was with Gideon, Micah, and Jeroboam,[1] infers at least an ancient disposition on the part of Israel towards such a representation. In this respect even the supposition that the image of God mentioned in Judg. viii. 27 was that of a bull, is just the point in question. Riehm[2] assumes that in Judg. viii. 27 the idea of the bull-image must be accepted because Dan, since Jeroboam's time, was one of the two towns noted for their calf-worship. Limited by the uncertain nature of the expression used, and by the close connection in which the image and the ephod in Judg. xviii. 18 are related to each other, it appears at least probable that the symbol of the Deity had here another form, being suited in its exterior for the use of the ephod. It resembled more the form of a pillar or a man. But also because the town of Dan was chosen by Jeroboam, it cannot exactly be decided that in Dan the image of a bull has been used since ancient times for the worship of Jahveh. No, if the choice of Dan as well as of Bethel cannot be explained from its geographical situation, but must be considered as arising from the old historical and religious signification of the town, we can only say, that in Dan from

---

[1] Ex. xxxii. 4 ; Judg. viii. 27, xvii. 3, xviii. 31 ; 1 Kings xii. 28.
[2] In the article "Bilderdienst" of his Handwörterbuch.

earliest times the honouring of Jahveh by image-worship was not only known but practised.

Graf Baudissin, taking advantage of the silence of the Old Testament regarding the idol-worship, asserts that the worship of the Deity through the image of a bull was native to Abraham and the Israelites. This, however, is an assertion ventured into without proof.[1] The phenomena to which he specially refers draw attention at least to the idea, which he seems to have revived, of representing Jahveh in the image of a bull. The bull-symbol, then, may be said to present itself to us in different aspects. In the wilderness wanderings it is regarded as a disposition on the part of the people to the worship of Egypt; by Jeroboam I., as a reminiscence of the image prepared by Aaron, which idea has been supported by the later recollections of the people.[2] In any circumstance, however, it comes

[1] Prot. Realencyclopädie, vii. (1880) p. 395 : "As the great ones of the earth were frequently represented by the image of a bull, and as especially the horn of a bull is the image or emblem of strength, accordingly, this representation does not despise the divine strength or the salvation proceeding from Him." . . . "It may still show that the Old Testament rite of the preparation of the water of separation from a red heifer arose from the old idea of the holiness of the calf" (Num. xix.). To this circumstance, however, surely no one can impute a reference to the Godhead being represented by such an image. Comp. my article "Reinigungen," in the Protest. Realencycl. xii. (1883) p. 633.

[2] The words recorded in 1 Kings xii. 28 seem to have been spoken by Jeroboam as well as Ezek. xvi. 26.

down as an inheritance in the legacy of thought and speech bequeathed to the people by their ancestors. We must also regard it as possible that the bull-symbol for Jahveh has till now been associated with the two sources referred to. We are compelled, however, with all scientific men who represent both answers given to this question, to declare against the origin of this bull-image as that which has been worked out by the Development Theorists.

While Gramberg[1] has regarded the idea of the bull representation of Jahveh as emanating from Egypt, we find Vatke,[2] on the other hand, asserting not only that this bull-symbol was indigenous to Israel, but Moses has not once forbidden its use.

First of all, Vatke lays great stress on the statement that Moses could not have wished to restrain the

[1] Kritische Geschichte der Religionsideen des A. T., i. (1829) p. 444: "To the Apis which they had worshipped in Egypt the Israelites, always prone to sensual worship, fashioned the image of a bull for the representation of Jahveh. This seems to have existed more as a private form of worship alongside of the worship enjoined by the covenant till Jeroboam I. brought it into use as that form of worship (only without an image) practised by the Court at Jerusalem. He thus made the worship of the Jahveh-Apis most powerful in Israel. This arose partly from the fact that already at Dan an image of Jahveh had previously been placed."

[2] Bibl. Theologie (1835) pp. 233-235, 266-272, 398, 403, 483 f.

people from such a representation of the Deity, because the ark of the covenant with its cherubim must have induced the people to such a corporeal representation of Jahveh. Further, he traces the command against idolatry as having its origin in the struggle against images, and in the recognition of the abstract ideal of God. And, lastly, the attitude assumed by idolatry towards the Mosaic Law seems to testify to a prohibition of the same. All this, however, does not stand the test of impartial criticism. The cherubim, for example, were not to represent Jahveh, in that Moses, as he laid down for the people, given into his charge by God, the foundations of religion and morality, fought against the natural tendency of Israel, which led them towards such a sensual representation of Jahveh. Moreover, the knowledge, not simply of the ideal being of God, but also of His spiritual essence, must of a truth be ascribed to Moses. While, finally, the prophets, who must ever be regarded as the best representatives of Jewish tradition, have not called in question the Mosaic origin of the commands against idol-worship.

In the second place, Vatke with a certain degree of confidence has accepted that exegesis which treats the ephod[1] as an image of Jahveh.[2] We, however, do not consider ourselves free to adopt this interpretation in such an offhand manner. It seems clear, by a reference for example to Isa. xxx. 22, that the word אֲפֻדָּה shows its verb אפד as generally used in a technical manner for law-making. From this we can only speak of the possibility that אפוד may signify a "covered image." And along with such a possibility there remains the certainty that אפוד signifies the loose upper garment of the high priest.

If, however, Vatke accepts the view that אפוד, in the passages of the Old Testament already referred to, with the Choschen (containing the Urim and Thummim), signifies the ordinary upper garment of the high priest, he must do so "on the supposition (by no means clear) of the great age of the high-priestly oracle." But we find that his representation of the comparatively recent origin of the intercession

---

[1] Judg. viii. 17, 18; 1 Sam. xxi. 10, xxiii. 6, 9, xxx. 7; Hos. iii. 4.

[2] For this see de Wette, Archäologie, 1st ed. (1814) § 228; Gesenius in Thesaurus Linguæ Hebr.; Gramberg, Krit. Gesch. der Religionsideen; Vatke and his followers; Kuenen in De Godsdienst, i. p. 102. Opposed to this interpretation are Thenius, Commentar zu 1 Sam. xxi. 10; Ewald, Alterthümer, 3rd ed. p. 298. Riehm in article on Ephod in his Handwörterbuch; Nowack, Commentar zu Hosea (1880); Bertheau, Buch der Richter und Ruth erklärt (1883), who defended his position with great success against Reuss. See also article "Ephod," in Prot. Real-Encycl. iv. p. 255, by Fr. Wilh. Schultz.

by the high priest before Jahveh carries him beyond the limits of his negative position. It was in opposition to the earlier idea of the Mosaic origin of public worship instituted even with its details in the Pentateuch, that the struggles of the prophets not only justified such a claim, but rendered it necessary. We find this position taken up by Vatke, supported further on by Stade. In his Geschichte des Volkes Israels, p. 92, he writes: " The high priest, at least in the sense ordinarily attached to the office, does not appear before the exodus. And the first priest in the temple was purely a royal official." In questioning such a statement, however, we would simply ask: What were Aaron, Eliezer, Phinehas, Eli in Shiloh, Ahimelech in Nob, and finally Abiathar, but the chief priests of Jahveh in Israel? For historical research, no matter how accurate it may be, can never reach to a certain knowledge of the fact as to Jahveh having been considered the chief lawgiver of the priests in Israel. These in their turn have regarded as their special mission the preserving and handing down of His law. And they on their part have supported the kingdom (as *e.g.* in Jehoiada's time), the kings being only secondary lawgivers when compared with the priests of Israel. This was so even when some of them went beyond the limits of their political sphere.

But, moreover, there must be satisfactory evidence at our disposal before we can conclude that the Israelites regarded the single word אֵפוֹד as containing the twofold signification of a covered image of Jahveh on the one hand, and the upper garment of the high priest on the other.

Among the representatives of the former of these views as to the exact signification of the word Ephod, Maybaum, *e.g.* in Die Entwickelung des Israelitischen Prophetenthums, 1883, p. 25, experienced the difficulty which lies in the fact that the word in question was used in old times to denote the divine image and the priestly dress. He, however, believes that he has removed this difficulty in the reference which he makes to Vatke's work. Vatke wrote (p. 269) that in the Book of Samuel when the priestly garment is mentioned, we find that it is designated by ephod, signifying as it does a linen garment (1 Sam. ii. 18, xxii. 18 ; 2 Sam. vi. 14). Only once does the word ephod there stand alone, and that is in 1 Sam. xiv. 3 in connection with the priest in Shiloh, who watches over the ark of the covenant. From this brief statement, however, we are not in a position to judge of any difference between the form and material of the ephod mentioned in 1 Sam. xiv. 3. For in this instance the priest occupied no superior relationship to the others, and the prerogative which the presence of the ark alone could give him was not of a permanent nature. It has not been affirmed either that an oracle-shield was fastened to his ephod ; on the other hand, the Scripture narrative is opposed to such a supposition (1 Sam. xiv.). Consequently, in Vatke's words we can only recognise the fact, as he himself

states it, that the word ephod, as one finds it in the
Books of Samuel, was used by a priest of Shiloh to
describe the priestly dress.[1] It seems almost incredible
that, from the fact of the priest in Shiloh wearing
the ephod, Vatke finds sufficient ground for explaining the omission of the "bath." He should
rather have emphasized the fact that Ahijah, the
head of the priesthood at Shiloh, was unquestionably
regarded as the ephod-bearer. Moreover, this priest,
as we see from the general narrative, is spoken of as
the means of communication and intercession between
God and Saul. Alongside of the Urim and Thummim
(spelt thamim by the Massoretes), which seemed to be
a sacred system of lots, there seem to have been other
means for guidance used by Saul. This, however, is
not apparent from the narrative. Lastly, the tradition
we possess cannot now be changed. For in these
three passages of Samuel, where we find mention
made of a "linen ephod," *e.g.* the child Samuel as he
ministers in the temple (1 Sam. ii. 18), the whole
company of 85 priests in Shiloh (1 Sam. xxii. 18),
and David (2 Sam. vi. 14), though not numbered
among the priests, are all alike spoken of as wearing
this garment.

Such a certain position cannot be found in the
mass of gold (1700 shekels) mentioned in Judg.

---

[1] This 14th chapter of 1 Sam., with some slight exceptions, can be
traced from the old sources of Samuel's writings. This is so with
ver. 3. Such a statement is supported even by the most advanced
critics. Comp. Bleek-Wellhausen, Einleitung in das A. T., § 104;
Stade, Geschichte Israeliten, pp. 215-219.

viii. 26. The ephod there referred to as prepared by Gideon may have been one of unusual splendour. It was not made of golden thread alone, for amongst the booty taken from the princes of Midian there is mention of purple (Judg. viii. 26). The use of the verb הִצִּיג (ver. 27) is even not significant, for in Judg. vi. 37 it is used in the description we there find of the wool stretched out on the thrashing-floor. Besides, according to the context,[1] the use of the ephod seems to have had in view the showing forth of the rule exercised by Jahveh over Israel. And the continual mediation,[2] as practised in theocratic Israel, was now the business of the priests in possession of the Urim and Thummim. Accordingly, from this connection it follows that Gideon, even while in Ophrah, made that garment which was to show forth with renewed power to the high priests at Shiloh the sovereignty of Jahveh.

We see, moreover, from a perusal of the 17th and 18th chapters of Judges that the writer regarded with special emphasis the ephod as a priestly garment. In looking into xvii. 4, 5, it appears to us

---

[1] Judg. viii. 23, 24–27.
[2] This is to be distinguished from the extraordinary mediation of the theocracy, which was granted through the prophets called forth by Jahveh at critical periods in the national history.

that Micah did not only possess a graven and a molten image, but a perfect sanctuary with all the necessary requisites; and he consequently provided a priestly ephod and teraphim, as well as a priest who should wear the ephod. The priest, however, amidst these sacred possessions is regarded as the most important of them all. Through him it is evident Micah and the Danites believed[1] their union with Jahveh to be made sure. On such a hypothesis, the writer appears to emphasize the fact of the ephod being necessary for the performance of the most important[2] priestly function. On which account also, with Abiathar,[3] the title "priest" was added, if at the consulting of the ephod he had only performed the services of an ordinary assistant, and had not rather been the person who wore the ephod, and who communicated the answer of Jahveh to the questions of David through the ordained manipulation of the Urim and Thummim. We might then find in the passages quoted from the Books of Judges and Samuel not quite conclusive traces of the religious-historical fact that a Gideon and a David had also worshipped their

---

[1] Judg. xvii. 13, xviii. 4, 5, 6, 19, 24, 30.
[2] At least so far as can be judged from the narrative.
[3] 1 Sam. xxiii. 9, xxx. 7.

Jahveh through a symbol. So we must conclude if we consider the passages quoted, but still more so if the pretended Jahveh-image of Gideon is said to have "probably possessed the form of a calf, or of a calf and of a man combined."[1] Now, if this supposition is to hold good, we ask, first, why, on the one hand, does not the word "ephod" occur in the description of the real representation of Jahveh under the form of a calf,[2] and why, on the other, in the religious rites of Gideon is there no reference to Egypt? But we ask, secondly, in how far the act of Jeroboam was regarded as a flagrant departure from the genuine religious tendencies of Israel as compared with the pretended calf-worship of David? These considerations are not at all superfluous, though they are opposed to a secondary hypothesis of Vatke's. On the other hand, they may be said to possess positive

---

[1] So Vatke judged, p. 268. Gramberg, i., had already energetically disputed that opinion (p. 448), nevertheless it has been accepted again by Kuenen in his Godsdienst, i. p. 235, as "very probable." Vatke even ventured on the assertion that "David's ephod had also, in all probability, the form of a calf." Then, according to him, the Israelitish historians must actually have forgotten to record the great service rendered by Solomon when he abolished from Israel's worship the calf symbols, to the adoration of which his father had given himself up! For a contradiction of such suppositions, see our preceding third and fourth inquiries.

[2] Ex. xxxii.–xxxiv. ; 1 Kings xii. 28.

interest, because they show that the doubtful interpretation of Gideon's ephod in the text (Judg. viii. 23–27) as an image of Jahveh is more doubtful when viewed in its religious-historical connection.[1]

But, thirdly, the idolatry introduced by Jeroboam is said to have been in reality only the beautifying of an older form of worship which had been preserved until then.[2] Kuenen[3] also says the opinion that an image of Jahveh had stood in the temple at Jerusalem was not only unproved but also very improbable, for in the place where it was expected the ark of Jahveh was found. In spite of that, however, he thinks that symbols which recalled the calf-worship, and which were evidently connected with it,[4] were not wanting in that temple. He maintains, therefore, that everything combines to prove the calf a national and original symbol of Jahveh. Duhm[5] also, in proof of

[1] Vatke himself emphasized it (ibid. p. 339) as "highly important that no Jahveh-image came into the temple of Solomon."

[2] So Vatke thought (ibid. p. 399), although he expressed the opinion in the preceding note regarding the absence of a Jahveh-image in Solomon's temple.

[3] De Godsdienst, i. p. 235.

[4] To the great altar where the daily offering was burnt there were four horns attached (1 Kings ii. 28), and the great laver, or so-called brazen sea, rested upon twelve oxen.

[5] Theologie der Propheten, p. 47, note 4.

the view that Jeroboam had returned to an "ancient and truly Hebrew form of worship,"[1] refers to the fact that "also in the temple of Solomon the calf-symbol played no mean part." But every sober consideration of history must recognise in the fact that the temple of Solomon (which, on thoroughly insufficient grounds,[2] has been called a temple of sun-worship [3]) contained no image of Jahveh. This in itself is an incontrovertible proof that the true worship of Jahveh knew no bodily representation.

Fourthly, a proof of the assertion that the symbolization of Jahveh by a calf, as introduced by Jeroboam, had been the legitimate Jahveh-worship of Israel, is said to lie in the fact that the controversy of Ahijah (1 Kings xiv. 9) was only the "utterance of the pragmatic views of a later time." This, we are told, is corroborated by the fact that "in the accounts of Elijah and Elisha no polemics against the calf-symbol

---

[1] "Which might have been dedicated indifferently to Jahveh or to Moloch, or whatever the deity was otherwise called."

[2] (Vatke, p. 336) Duhm, p. 53: "The two pillars before the entrance, the carving on the walls, the palms and flowers for which the mason-work could not be seen, the pomegranates on the pillars, all these were also to be found in the Phœnician temples, and did not only represent a view (side) of the Godhead, but also the presence of the Divine Being in nature."

[3] Vatke has had this designation printed in large type, p. 337, and Duhm (p. 52) emphasized it as a new truth.

are mentioned."[1] The authenticity of the narrative of the unknown Jewish prophets (1 Kings xiii.) certainly seems so doubtful[2] that the relation of Ahijah's influence on the course (events) of history may also be considered an invention, although the older historical books of Israel cannot be regarded as so untrustworthy.[3] Further, with regard to the silence of Elijah and Elisha as pointed out by Vatke, in the first place, their polemics against the calf-worship required to be no constant element of their prophetic activity; secondly, we find both prophets, which is very remarkable, at work, not at Bethel nor at Dan, but wandering rather to Horeb;[4] thirdly, they had a worse error of their contemporaries than the adoration of Jahveh images to contend with, viz. the threatened falling away, since the time of Ahab and Jezebel, of the masses of Israel to the worship of false gods.

[1] "Which, with the comprehensiveness of those accounts, would be a conspicuous feature, if that controversy had formed a striking and constant element of prophetic activity." Vatke, ibid. p. 400 f.

[2] Because that prophet is anonymous, and on account of the mention of the name Josiah.

[3] See pp. 27 ff. for the proof.

[4] Even if the supposition of Hävernick (Einleitung in d. A. T., ii. 2, p. 23) and Oehler (Theologie des A. T., § 174 [English translation of both published by T. & T. Clark, Edinburgh]), that the faithful worshippers of Jahveh among the Ten Tribes assembled round the prophets as round a living central-point of worship and a substitute for the temple, were not sufficiently founded.

The assertion that the true prophets of the kingdom of the Ten Tribes had regarded the image-worship of Jahveh as lawful, will appear impossible from a glance at the oldest Scripture prophets. For even the evolution theorists do not attempt to deny[1] that Amos[2] and Hosea (viii. 5, xiii. 2) expressly designated the symbolization of Jahveh by the image of a calf as apostasy from the true worship, as a culpable offence, and the reason of their exile (Amos vii. 11, 17). How then is the pretended difference to be explained which is said to exist between Elijah and Elisha on the one hand, and Amos, etc., on the other hand, with regard to the attitude they observed concerning the image-worship of Jahveh?[3] It[4] is answered that this difference of attitude in the prophets arises from the fact that in the course of the centuries following on Jeroboam I. idolatrous elements[5] had entered the image-worship of Jahveh, or that the worship of

---

[1] See Vatke, p. 401 ; Kuenen, De Godsdienst, i. p. 79 f. Stade in his Zeitschrift für die alttestamentliche Wissenschaft, 1883, p. 9 f.

[2] iv. 4, v. 5, vii. 9 ff., viii. 14.

[3] Maybaum himself has not ventured to draw any direct conclusion from his opinion that the prophets, since Samuel's time, regarding themselves as agents of revelation filled with the Holy Ghost, were withheld from the adoration of the Jahveh images (Die Entwickelung des israelitischen Prophetenthmus, 1883, p. 49).

[4] Vatke, ibid. p. 402 f.

[5] As the kissing of the calf images. Hos. xiii. 2; comp. 1 Kings xix. 18.

Jahveh with that of idols was freely combined. This attempt at an explanation, which besides would not make the assumed difference in the attitude of the prophets a fact, can, by a free exegesis of the Old Testament, be considered as little successful as the endeavour to prove, firstly, in addition to the calf symbols, still other traces of legal image-worship of Jahveh, and secondly, in Hosea, Isaiah, and Micah, additional evidence for the natural development of Israel's religion. It has been contended,[1] firstly, that the Mosaic authority of the prohibition of image-worship is contradicted by the figures of the cherubim[2] upon the ark, because through these things the people might have concluded that Jahveh might be represented to the senses. Kuenen adds[3] that the opinion that Jahveh was Himself present in the ark gives evidence of a sensual conception of His being. Nevertheless, it is clear how little demonstrative power that argument can claim. For, in the first place, Moses could not be held responsible if subsequent generations regarded the cherubim as representations of Jahveh, and this later view of the people could not prove that Moses had conceived a representation of Jahveh in

---

[1] Vatke, ibid. p. 233 f.   [2] De Godsdienst, i. p. 232 f.
[3] If both are traced from Moses.

the giving of the fundamental moral law to Israel. Secondly, it cannot be deduced from the Israelites' belief in the presence of Jahveh among the cherubim that they were ignorant of the impossibility of representing their God, and had misapprehended His spirituality.

Further, Kuenen,[1] in his endeavour to make the Mosaic origin of the prohibition of image-worship appear improbable, asserts as historical facts that "that interdict destroys the connection between the ten commandments,[2] that image-worship was the state religion among the Ten Tribes, that a grandson of Moses acted as priest to an image of Jahveh, and, lastly, that Moses himself prepared the brazen serpent." But that the extension of the ten commandments in their totality, their compass, and their nature did not necessarily originate with Moses can be calmly asserted. If, moreover, in spite of the prohibition of idol-worship, acknowledged as ancient even by Kuenen, Solomon reverenced other gods besides Jahveh, then Jeroboam might also transgress the command. If Aaron complied with the wish of the people to possess a visible representation of God, so

---

[1] De Godsdienst, i. p. 283 f.
[2] This name is found in Ex. xxxiv. 28 ; Deut. iv. 13, x. 4.

might also a grandson of Moses (Judg. xviii. 30) in a case of need take up his position before a sanctuary furnished with images. Finally, how can we conclude, with Kuenen, from the mention of the brazen serpent (2 Kings xviii. 4), that "Moses was not so opposed to images as the Pentateuch represents him, or, at least, that the people who made the brazen serpent an object of adoration knew nothing [1] of a prohibition so express as it appears in the decalogue?" Yet, if in 2 Kings xviii. 4 nothing more is said than that the Israelites burnt incense to the brazen serpent, consequently regarding it as an object of reverential fear but not as a representation of Jahveh, and if the same passage states at the same time that this lower worship was condemned by the clearer insight of Isaiah and his pious disciple Hezekiah, who represented the genuine tradition, then the brazen serpent would cease to be brought up as an argument against the Mosaic authority of the prohibition of image-worship.

Neither is the adoration of the teraphim as possessed by Micah, and even by David [2] himself, an argument of that kind. For such a household god, which was considered a promoter of the wellbeing

---

[1] De Godsdienst, i. pp. 284, 285.   [2] Judg. xvii. 5 ; 1 Sam. xix. 13.

of a family, was not meant to represent Jahveh Himself, but rather a πνεῦμα λειτουργικόν—one of His angels.

Secondly, we come now to speak of the fact that some have lately thought themselves able to prove from Hosea, Isaiah, and Micah what might be traces of the natural growth of the Israelitish religion. Whilst Vatke,[1] Kuenen,[2] Duhm[3] admitted that Hezekiah's reform (2 Kings xviii. 4, 22) extended to the מַצֵּבָה and the אֲשֵׁרָה as well as to the Jahveh images,[4] it has lately been called in question by

---

[1] Ibid. p. 482, note 3, whilst he compares Isa. xvii. 3.
[2] De Godsdienst, i. pp. 86 f., 408 f.
[3] Theologie der Propheten, p. 195.
[4] Vatke (p. 483) tried in the following manner to make it appear "highly probable, indeed as good as certain," that Jahveh images were also found in the high places (Bamoth of Judah). He says: "Judah was full of idols, therefore there must have been Jahveh images among them, for Jahveh must have been considered by the greater number of the people, even by the idolaters, as the mightiest or, at least, as a very powerful god, whose protection they sought to procure. Now, if that took place by means of idols which were worshipped as visible gods, it is incomprehensible that Jahveh should not have been included in the number, or rather *according to the pattern of the temple symbols*, that He should have been quite separate from it." Kuenen in his Godsdienst, i. p. 86, thinks it "very possible, indeed even probable," that the images, of whose use Isaiah and Micah complain, were in part Jahveh images. He omits the appeal to Isa. ii. 8, and indeed it must be maintained that Isaiah did not mean Jahveh images by the word elohim. So the assumption that Jahveh images were worshipped in Judah also must be regarded as unfounded, for the prophets did not combat false Jahveh-worship, but idolatry.

Stade[1] whether Hezekiah's reform included the abolishment of the brazen serpent and the Jahveh images,[2] as it only affected the objects of prophetic renunciation, the prophets "having found no fault with the מַצֵּבָה and the אֲשֵׁרָה[3]—those rites of ancient Israelitish worship which had grown out of the adoration of representations of nature, of stone and tree worship."

This last assertion, although there would seem to be some foundation for it in Hos. iii. 4 f., is yet incorrect. For certainly it seems as if things, which are withdrawn from their possessor as a means of punishment, must be regarded as his lawful possessions; but if even logic does not demand this consequence, yet in

[1] In the Zeitschrift für die alttestl. Wissenschaft (1883), pp. 9-14, edited by him.

[2] Which also Stade, ibid. p. 10, believes to have been, "according to Isaiah, in the hands of many private persons."

[3] This word is used here by Stade in that sense in which it is the symbol of Astarte. He used it in the sense in which it is the synonym of Astarte in his Zeitschrift (1881), p. 345, "dismissed from the Semitic Pantheon." Besides this, Budde (Theol. Literaturzeitung (1884), col. 213 f.) infers that the Aschera was not so much joined to the worship of Astarte as to that of Baal. He refers to the similarity and feminine form of both words, but with so weighty reasons opposed he cannot find in these sufficient proof to justify their connection. But we may ask what are these weighty reasons? Does not Baal find his symbol elsewhere? Does not the evergreen erected before the eye suggest the idea or symbol of the goddess of fruitfulness? Is tradition to be regarded as of no value? (Comp. Schrader, Keilinschriften und Altes Testament, 2 Aufl. (1883) p. 178 f.)

the case[1] before us it is forbidden by the nearer circumstances of the text. For among the possessions withheld from the Ten Tribes during the time of their punishment was that kingdom which originated[2] in rebellion, and which was to be restored to the house of David—that princely family in favour with God.[3] However unlawful the first possession of the Ten Tribes condemned to captivity is, then if the connection of thought is to be a natural one, the other possessions must be equally so. Such a conclusion must be drawn from the positive element of the text as well as from its negative side. It is not said that the Ten Tribes were to return from exile to the elements of their present worship, but that they should seek Jahveh as their God and strive reverently after His blessing. The law of antithesis[4] even asserts that the things mentioned above are not regarded by

---

[1] By this I rectify a phrase which occurs in the literary criticism contained in my Offenbarungsbegriff des A. T., ii. p. 326. It seemed doubtful to me then, and I therefore added the word "moreover." My views as a literary-historical critic do not, however, depend on that phrase.

[2] Kuenen has also correctly recalled that fact. De Godsdienst, i. p. 82.

[3] As a God-pleasing family it experienced the favour of God, and was so far not the support of the whole earthly kingdom of Israel. Comp. Inquiry X.

[4] Offerings, pillars, the shoulder garments and household gods.

Hosea as elements of the worship of Jahveh, for otherwise it could not be said that turning from these things the children of the Ten Tribes should seek Jahveh. Hosea did not regard the sacrifice as an absolutely necessary and truly essential expression of Israelitish piety (Hos. vi. 6, ix. 4).[1] Further, the מַצֵּבָה are also named as parts of the idolatrous worship denounced by Hosea (x. 1 f.); for the children of the Ten Tribes did not fear Jahveh (ver. 3), and the calves of "Bethaven"[2] are not understood as images of Jahveh, but as idols.

If, further, Isa. xix. 19 is to be considered the only passage in the Old Testament which proves that pillars were raised at the altars built to Jahveh, then it ought plainly to contain that statement. But whilst the altar of Jahveh is said to have stood in the midst of the land of Egypt, the pillar is said to have been raised on the borders of Egypt in order to announce the land of Egypt to strangers as a territory consecrated to Jahveh.[3]

Stade attempts to set aside the evidence of Isaiah

---

[1] Nowack points out these passages as opposed, in his opinion, to the preceding exposition (Der Prophet Hosea ausgelegt (1880), p. 48).

[2] Which "Bethel" had become (Hos. x. 5).

[3] The words "all the heathen who are called by my name" (Amos ix. 12) are a more distant parallel.

xvii. 8, which is opposed to his thesis, by expunging the word "altars" from the first half of the verse, and the "asherahs and sun-pillars" from the second half. As a justification of the erasure, he maintains that the altars were unquestionably the work of the hand of man, so that this expression originates not with the prophet himself, but with a verbose commentator. In our opinion, however, the detail in question may, notwithstanding, have been emphasized by the prophet himself when he denounced the unnatural trust which the Israelites placed in the altars. Besides, we are prevented from agreeing with Stade through the circumstance that the acceptation of "altars" as a gloss is the more difficult, because in that case a reader could much less easily discover the altar to be the object meant by Isaiah. Consequently the passage contained in Micah v. 12, which also contradicts the historical assertion of Stade, and is set aside by him as a post-Isaiahic insertion, need not be regarded as belonging to any other period than the Isaiahic.

But—so Stade says—there stood, even in Josiah's time, an asherah in the temple at Jerusalem (2 Kings xxiii. 6), and, he warns us, we are not to imagine that it was again erected in the temple under Manasseh! This is doing violence to the historians of the Old

Testament, for it is not without historical grounds that they describe Hezekiah as a comparatively faithful worshipper of Jahveh, but Manasseh as an apostate prince (2 Kings xxi. 2 f.[1]). So the reaction of Manasseh's reign, which followed Hezekiah's reformation, must be taken into account if the history of Judaic Jahveh-worship is to be represented in accordance with the truth of its proved traditions, and not built upon unlimited negation.

Neither is it to be assumed that the command issued in Deuteronomy to remove the pillars and asheras of the Canaanites (or rather those borrowed from them by the Israelites) was without a bearing on the time when it was issued. On the contrary, it is much more probable that the ideal perfection and purification of Jahveh-worship which, since the eighth century, had been taking a more and more clear definition in the preaching of the prophets, and had found a partial realization through Hezekiah, were

---

[1] A criticism of the Old Testament which disregards such limits defeats its own ends. It can be as little accepted as the chronological theory of Krey, Wellhausen, and Stade. With regard to the chronology of the time of the Israelitish kings, that has been proved in our Beiträgen zur Biblischen Chronologie (Zeitschrift für kirchliche Wissenschaft und kirchl. Leben (1883), pp. 456-458), and at the same time by Kamphausen (Die Chronologie der hebräischen Könige, Bonn 1883).

ascribed to Moses by the author of Deuteronomy as the form of Mosaic principles necessary to the restoration of the pure Mosaic form of Jahveh-worship.

So, then, exegesis has shown in its answer to such a question, that only that is to be considered a departure from the pre-prophetic and Mosaic worship (views ?) of God which is judged as such in the Old Testament itself.[1]

[1] Holy mountains, trees, and stones as they appear in the time subsequent to Moses do not violate the spirituality of Jahveh. (As fresh information on that subject, compare Guthe's communications in his notes on Palästina in Bild und Wort, i. p. 504, ii. p. 449.)

CHAPTER IX.

Was there in Jahvism a development of views regarding the moral character of Jahveh?—It sounded like irony when Daumer[1] and Ghillany[2] treated in a special chapter " the moral side of Jahveh." For they meant rather the immorality of the God[3] of the Old Testament. We do not need to quote and contradict singly the arguments of these two scholars, as that Old Testament interpretation which seems at least to justify that judgment of the God of Israel is also supported by the most moderate evolution theorists. For they have supported the criticism on the God of ancient Israel contained in Ghillany's statement that the pre-prophetic Jahveh acted with violence, if not

---

[1] Ibid. pp. 4-18.   [2] Ibid. pp. 373-429.
[3] Ghillany begins (p. 373) with the sentence : "The predominant quality of the Israelitish God is a terrible, furious disposition (temperament), also seen in the spirit of the reformers of the period subsequent to the captivity. The Jahveh of the time before the captivity had probably a milder, generic side, but of that only faint traces remain to us."

I

capriciously or despotically, that He dealt according to the scale of external greatness, that as the source of physical life He exacted from His creatures the renunciation of life, or at least of bodily health, that "often the might of Jahveh or His inclination to reveal it exceeded the demands of justice," and that "power was the most conspicuous of His qualities."[1] The arguments which Kuenen employs in support of these assertions are the following:—

Firstly, the opinion has always been generally accepted,[2] that even from the pre-prophetic polemics it can be pointed out that human sacrifice was a national custom observed in the worship of Jahveh;[3] and that as Micah "did not utter his own words or borrow them from another form of nature-worship," then, according to him, "the offering of a human sacrifice in his days could not have been regarded as preposterous."

But the passages in the prophecy alluded to must be judged as follows:—Even if the prophet had

[1] Kuenen, De Godsdienst, i. pp. 221, 233, 236-241; Volksreligion und Weltreligion, pp. 116, 119.

[2] Not only by Daumer, ibid. p. 51, but also by Vatke, ibid. p. 276, by Kuenen, De Godsdienst, i. pp. 221, 236, and also by Maybaum, Die Entwickelung des israelit. Prophetenthums, 1883, p. 99.

[3] Micah vi. 7: "Shall I give my first-born for my transgression, the fruit of my body for the sin of my soul?"

wished to combat the opinion of certain of the children of Israel, that Jahveh could be conciliated by the sacrifice of children, that opinion would have been pointed out by the prophet as one contrary to the expressed commands of Jahveh (Deut. iv. 8). That opinion then would not be represented as one of the elements of the legitimate religion dating from Moses. But it is not to be even assumed that Micah wished to oppose the theory of any Israelites that human sacrifices ought and should be offered to Jahveh. Rather, since immediately before (in ver. 5) mention is made of the Moabitish king, it is tolerably clear that Micah wrote to remind his contemporaries of the sad traditional fact[1] that the King of Moab had sacrificed his first-born son,[2] and that after, if not on account of that deed, the army of Israel sustained a defeat.[3] That[4] Hosea (xiii. 2) reproaches the calf-worshippers of the Ten Tribes with their human sacrifices as the most flagrant departure from the true worship of Jahveh, we cannot accept, because the sole and entire emphasis of the prophet's discourse rests, not upon human sacrifice, but upon the image-worship

---

[1] 2 Kings iii. 27.   [2] Exactly as Micah says (Micah vi. 7).
[3] See Hitzig-Steiner's Die Kleinen Propheten erklärt (1880), z. St. ; Kleinert in Lange's Bibelwerk (1868), z. St.
[4] Kuenen's De Godsdienst, i. p. 180 f.

of Jahveh described in detail, and including the kissing of the calves. In order to refute the interpretation advanced by Kuenen, we do not need to refer to the fact that such a horrible institution as human sacrifice, appearing, as it does, in the Old Testament in its full reality and not in a figurative sense, could not have been mentioned by Hosea as a natural element of the worship of Jahveh. The form of expression, זבחי אדם, which occurs in the passage in question, is, in our opinion, intended to represent the generalized *Relativum*. The passage ought therefore to be re-written thus: "Each one who comes to the sacrifice, to the performance of worship, to prove by deeds his reverence for Jahveh, takes part in the kissing of the calf images."

Secondly, we cannot feel convinced that we are told in Judg. xi. 31–40 of the literal sacrifice, that is to say, the slaying and burning[1] of Jephthah's daughter; for although the terms of the vow (ver. 31)

---

[1] This is the opinion not only of the evolutionists (such as Vatke, p. 275 f.; Kuenen, De Godsdienst, i. p. 237), but also of most other theologians, such, for instance, as Von Diestel in Richm's Handwörterbuch, p. 671; Herr Schultz, Alttestl. Theol., p. 118; Oehler's Alttestl. Theol., § 159; Bertheau, das Buch der Richter erklärt, 1883, pp. 193–198. But the view which seems to me the most correct has also had its supporters lately, such, for instance, as Köhler, Lehrbuch der Bibl. Geschichte, ii. (1877) p. 102; Cassel in his article on "Jephthah," in the Protest. Realencycl. vi. (1879) p. 513.

seem to require that interpretation, yet the actual (positive) sense of the oath must be decided by the manner of its fulfilment. Now it is not related that Jephthah's daughter bewailed her life but her virginity; and the close of the narrative, " she knew no man," seems to us not to affirm her virginity, but to require the interpretation that her sacrifice consisted[1] in her consecration as a vestal to the service of Jahveh.[2]

Thirdly, we are not required to believe from the Old Testament that human beings were offered to Jahveh for the purpose of satisfying or propitiating Him, even in cases of departure from the legitimate religion. It is inconceivable how any one can appeal[3] to Jer. xix. 5,[4] in order to prove the proposition just refuted. For there we read that children were offered in sacrifice to Baal alone. It is therefore of the highest importance for scriptural history that the only

[1] See 1 Sam. ii. 22; Ex. xxxviii. 8; comp. also "male offerings," Num. xxxi. 28, 30, etc.

[2] Our opinion on that single point is a secondary matter. Bertheau correctly describes Jephthah's oath (ibid. p. 198) as one which was regarded by the narrator himself as "extraordinary," and therefore exceeding the normal religious views of ancient Israel. But we did not wish to pass over in silence the exegesis which the text seems to us to demand.

[3] Even Diestel in Riehm's Handwörterbuch, p. 671.

[4] "And they (your fathers) have built also the high places of Baal, to burn their sons with fire for burnt-offerings unto Baal, which I commanded not nor spake it, neither came it into my mind."

instance in which a human sacrifice is mentioned as being offered "to Jahveh" is spoken of by the Gibeonites (2 Sam xxi. 6), whilst the Israelitish historian, in describing the execution of the Gibeonites' proposal (intention?), uses the ordinary expression "before Jahveh" (ver. 9), which is also found in 1 Sam. xv. 33.

Therefore the conclusion[1] that these words are used to denote sacrifice is incorrect. No, in spite of the "before Jahveh," or rather, just because it and not the dative is used, Agag was not offered as a sacrifice. His death had only a negative relation to Jahveh, or, in other words, through His death the negative side of Israel's relation to other races, arising from its position as a chosen people, made itself known, viz. hatred of all enemies of Jahveh and His people; whilst in the sacrifices the positive side of Israel's election (?) found expression,[2] viz. Israel's reverence for Jahveh's thoughts and views. So Israelitish tradition preserved the correct religious consciousness,[3] when it ascribed to the first representative of

---

[1] Daumer, ibid. pp. 26 f., 29, note; and Kuenen, De Godsdienst, i. p. 237; and even Herm. Schultz, Alttestl. Theologie, p. 152.

[2] Or should find.

[3] The opinion that the Old Testament historians correctly estimated the antiquity of Israel's fundamental theological views has been supported not only by general principles (p. 18), but also by special proofs.

Israel's religious peculiarity the departure from the barbarous stages of worship, the human sacrifice (Gen. xxii.). Or might not this narrative simply prove, on the contrary, that human sacrifices were considered by the narrator as "possibly lying within the sphere of Jahveh-worship," or as "possibly commanded[1] by Him"? No, in both the suppositions here quoted the extent of criticism permitted by the nature of the Old Testament is exceeded. For how could it be maintained that everything which is mentioned as a thing abhorred or forbidden by Jahveh must be considered as an institution which actually existed in the earlier phases of the development of His own worship, or in Israel's manner of life, and which was now sought to be suppressed in the advance of civilisation? Are not most of the institutions displeasing to Jahveh described as peculiar to the worship of strange gods, and occurring among foreign races? Is it not expressly said that the Israelites, *turning away from Jahveh*, sacrificed their children to Baal, or Moloch, or to strange gods in general?[2] The fact just stated, that human sacrifices are mentioned as the peculiar

---

[1] Vatke, ibid. p. 276 ; Kuenen, De Godsdienst, i. p. 237.

[2] To Baal, according to Jer. xix. 5, 2 Kings xxi. 3-6 ; to Moloch, Jer. xxxii. 35, 2 Kings xxiii. 10 ; to strange gods in general, according to Ezek. xvi. 20 (lahém), xxiii. 37 (to their idols), 2 Kings xvi. 3.

attribute of idolatrous worship, and that consequently the Old Testament contains a positive prohibition of human sacrifice in Israel, is the strongest argument against the theory that the Israelites regarded such sacrifices as reconcilable with the character of Jahveh. The inadmissibility of that opinion would become still more evident if the question were asked, How is it possible that Israel could have fallen away from Jahveh to Moloch, and that with the erection of the altars to Moloch (1 Kings xi. 7) a new phase began in the religion of Israel, if the sacrificing of children was held consistent with the character of the true God of Israel, and if such offerings had been made to Him until the commencement of that new phase?

This utter impossibility is not made more probable by Ezek. xx. 25, and we believe that we can put an end to the disputes to which that passage has given rise,[1] for we are firmly convinced that Ezekiel never thought that his words could be supposed to have reference to human sacrifices. The prophet shows that he had not thought of the offering of the human first-born through the negative force of the argument that according to him children were sacrificed only to

[1] Comp. Kurtz, Geschichte des Alten Bundes, ii. pp. 419-421.

monsters and idols (blocks of wood?), but that Jahveh had given no directions to the Israelites to serve other gods besides Him.[1] What he meant by a false sacrifice of the first-born is shown by the positive argument contained in ver. 26, and expressed by the words, "I polluted them." For it is a fact[2] that in Ezekiel particularly the desire (interest!) for religious-moral purity attains fuller expression than in any of the preceding Old Testament writers. Therefore the only possible interpretation[3] seems indicated by the choice of the verb, namely, that Israel, in offering the first-born, sinned through neglect of the limits existing between clean and unclean animals.[4]

But have we not direct evidence that until the time

---

[1] So we must not think, with Smend (Der Prophet Ezekiel erklärt (1880), z. St.), that the prophets believed the sacrifice of the first-born child to be an old custom in Israel. That view arose rather from the calumnious reports of the heathen, envious of the religious and historical peculiarity of Israel. Comp. Josephus, contra Apionem, 2. 7. 8.

[2] Comp. our proofs of this and of its origin in our article "Reinigungen," in der Protestantischen Realencycl. xii. (1883) pp. 618-637.

[3] Because, according to the negative argument already stated, human sacrifices could not possibly have been meant for the legitimate God of Israel.

[4] A complaint similar to that of Hos. ix. 4; Mal. i. 12-14. The question what ordinances of Jahveh are described by Ezekiel as not good does not belong to this part of our researches, and shall therefore only be answered by annotation. As sacrifices of children (which were wrongly offered to Jahveh) are not meant, then the command given in Ex. xxii. 29: "The first-born of thy sons shalt thou give to me,"

of Moses at least, the sacrifice of the first-born was customary in Israel? Is not the statement that the first-born in Israel were consecrated to the service of Jahveh because of the passing over of the destroying angel in Egypt, and that they had afterwards to be redeemed from that service by the substitution of the Levites, only a false explanation of the ancient law that the first-born were the special servants of the national God? The representation that Moses' abolishment of child-sacrifice is an established fact, suppressed[1] in Israelitish tradition, that the story of the sparing of Israel's first-born in Egypt was invented as a reason for that abolishment, and that therefore the reason for the fiction disappeared from history whilst the fiction

signifies only: "Sanctify unto me all the first-born," etc. (Ex. xiii. 2). This statute is called "not good," because in the wording of it no difference is made between clean and unclean animals, and it therefore caused the Israelites to dedicate also unclean first-born to their God. The prophet believed that Jahveh, by such generally (indefinitely) expressed statutes, wished to put His people to the proof, in order to see if they would understand of themselves that the first-born of clean animals might be sacrificed directly to the holy God, but that unclean animals could only be offered indirectly, that is, through redemption or by the offering of an equivalent. Therefore there is no such contradiction as Smend maintains between Ezekiel's conception of Jahveh's purpose in issuing that general command (Ex. xiii. 2) and the declaration of Jeremiah (vii. 31, xix. 5), that Jahveh did not desire the sacrifice of children with regard to His own worship as they were offered by Israel to Baal.

[1] Vatke, ibid. pp. 198, 489; Kuenen, De Godsdienst, i. 239.

itself remained, also appears to us too artificial. We do not think it possible to doubt the correctness of Israelitish tradition so far as to assume that there was no real foundation for the narrative of the destruction of the first-born in Egypt. We think we may at least suppose that the eldest son of the Egyptian king was carried off by sudden illness, and that this blow, acting as the final link in the chain of calamities which befell the Egyptians at the time when Moses was endeavouring to obtain the release of his brethren, was the means of gaining from the Egyptian government a temporary assent to their departure.

Finally, circumcision is represented as a substitute for child-sacrifice.[1] But this view cannot be founded even upon Ex. iv. 24–26. For if, according to the narrative, that had been Zipporah's view, she would have rejoiced and not grieved at such an application of the ordinance. In the passage quoted, therefore, circumcision cannot be regarded as a substitute for a worse custom, but as an independent institution, having its own ends,[2] and one which seemed to Zipporah, as

---

[1] Kuenen, De Godsdienst, i. p. 238.

[2] Namely, to mark out the men of Israel, and through them the whole of the people, as a (priestly) nation dedicated to God. This refutes Kuenen's observation (ibid.), that among other races circumcision was performed only by the priests.

well as to mothers in general, a dangerous[1] observance. It appears to us that this interpretation of the passage in Exodus in its present connection[2] gives the true meaning of the Israelitish tradition, and is also correct according to the text itself.

But even if it were granted that pre-Mosaic Israel believed child-sacrifice to be pleasing to God, and that even Abraham, for the greater part of his life, had thought it reconcilable with the character of his God, yet we could not conclude from that, as the evolutionists do, as to the moral, natural, physical, and essentially different character of the God of the patriarchs. We only gather from the idea of child-sacrifice, the fact that former races cherished a false idea both of the degree and manner in which guilty humanity, in need of atonement, should consecrate itself to God, and of the capability of ordinary human beings to satisfy the Divine Being through self-sacrifice.[3]

---

[1] Comp. Palmer, Der Schauplatz der Wustenwanderung (1876), p. 74.

[2] Dillmann also considers this very probable, Exodus und Leviticus erklärt (1880), z. St.

[3] This last sentence must be added because the supposed human sacrifices of Old Testament Jahvism have been made use of by vulgar rationalists as well as by evolutionists to represent the God-man as the consequence of an unworthy conception of God on the part of the Jews, which sacrifice was yet necessary (Rom. iii. 25 f.) to meet the requirements of justice, and could be offered (Ps. xlix. 8 f.) by incarnate holiness (John iii. 19).

The assertion that "Israel began gradually to borrow traits from the character of the benevolent Baal in order to depict that of the mighty destructive Deity Jahveh, and that by that means the representation of the latter became a milder one," is therefore altogether unfounded.[1] As the consciousness of the difference between the national God of Israel and the god of the Canaanites is shown in a marked manner throughout the whole of Old Testament tradition, it cannot be supposed that the conception of Jahveh was combined with characteristics of the heathen deity.

Not only do we find an incomprehensible difference between "moral qualities ascribed to Jahveh by the people and a moral character by the canonical prophets,"[2] but we must also protest against that conception of Jahveh's holiness which is principally to be found in that part of the Old Testament theology on which our present researches are intended to cast light.

(a) The old incorrect extreme is certainly not avoided by Delitzsch[3] when he says: "The holiness of God consists in His freedom from every physical

---

[1] Tiele, Compendium (1880), § 54.
[2] Kuenen, Volksreligion und Weltreligion, p. 115.
[3] Article "Holiness," in the Protestant. Realencycl. v. p. 718.

imperfection; He is called holy, not as the heavenly, preternaturally sublime, excellent, unapproachable, incomparable One; these are the radii of the conception, not its centrum." For when Delitzsch can maintain that also in Ex. xv. 6, 11, Josh. xxiv. 19, 1 Sam. ii. 2, vi. 20, the ethic colouring of holiness is not absent, so then the admission that קֹדֶשׁ signifies "sublimity" is involved through the acknowledgment which he made (p. 714)[1] regarding the etymology of קדש, defended by Count Baudissin.[2] For if קדש[3] is not derived from "to be light," but signifies from its root קד, "separate," then a general extension must be given to it; it must be interpreted as God's separation from all that is not divine, and holiness must be "sublimity," including moral and ethical perfection as its most important element. Also when Delitzsch emphasizes physical completeness as an element of holiness, he includes in that holiness the vivifying power and omnipotence. This idea is undoubtedly an after-effect of Diestel's treatise[4] in which holiness was defined as "normality of life."

---

[1] Renouncing his former opinion.
[2] Studien zur Semitischen Religionsgeschichte, ii. (1878) pp. 1-42. Der Begriff der Heiligkeit im A. T.
[3] As Delitzsch formerly believed.
[4] The "Holiness of God," in the Jahrbücher für Deutsche Theologie (1859), pp. 3-43.

(β) The correct conception of holiness is the following: A correct examination of the etymology of קדש shows that Count Baudissin has deduced too much [1] from the Israelites' custom of language (manner of speech ?). He ought only to have concluded that which his former considerations had led him to believe, viz. that the idea of purity was combined with the derivation of קדש. Although two words such as קדש (holy) and טהור (pure) may appear in a language as antitheses, yet the difference between them is not necessarily an absolute, but a relative one. Or, to express it more clearly, the two ideas may be opposed to each other, not because their meaning is entirely different, but because the signification of the one is more comprehensive than that of the other. Now what the logical development asserts is confirmed by the fact that the signification of קדש comprehends not only absolute separation, but also purity; whilst טהור expresses the last-named quality alone. If, then, the holiness of God is only separation from all imperfection,

---

[1] Ibid. That the signification of קדש is not "purity," but rather implies the idea of "separation," is permissible from the general use of the words; this, in so far as there is a distinction between קדש and טהור—the latter being contrasted with חל. As a contrast to טהור the term טמא, signifying "impure" or "unclean," is used. (Amos ii. 7; 1 Sam. xxi. 5; Ezek. xxii. 26, xlii. 20, xliv. 23; Lev. x. 10.)

and is therefore sublimity, it is especially sublimity to what is morally objectionable, simply because what is ungodly is immoral to the religious man, and to the unperverted mind morality is the preponderating factor in the perfect state of free, pure beings. The holiness of God, then, is His self-appertainment founded on His moral and ethic perfection; and if human holiness denotes only relation to God, yet that excludes the conscious and intentional trespass of divine law. With man, then, holiness is the appertainment to the Divine Being on the ground of his objective blamelessness as ordained by God, and his endeavours after subjective moral perfection.

(γ) The source of the new extreme definition of the idea "holiness" may be described as follows:—Only when it is considered in its limited sense can it appear as if "holiness" were a morally indifferent conception. As Count Baudissin has examined the Old Testament view of holiness from the sacred objects (mentioned there?), he has not quite escaped the danger in question. For he says, ibid. p. 131: "The two significations of קדוש, namely, first, 'sublime' or 'heavenly,' and second, 'pure,' are not far removed from each other, and perhaps the apparent primary conception has never existed alone." Notwithstanding, he thinks (p. 132) that the holiness of God mentioned in 2 Sam. xxiv. 1 could not have meant sinlessness. Yet there it says: "And again the anger of the Lord was kindled against Israel, and He moved David against them to say, 'Go, number Israel and Judah,'" which, of course, does not imply a sin on the part of Jahveh, but rather a consequence of His anger. Therefore that passage does not prevent its author from regarding the sinlessness of God as the most important element of His holiness. The second Isaiah also, who highly extols the holiness of God,[1] describes Jahveh as the author of evil as well as of good, the former being a punishment or means of purifying mankind.

Still more unfounded, and still more at variance with the Old Testament, is the judgment of Herm. Schultz,[2] that "Holiness was the consuming splendour, therefore not a moral, but a mental conception. The creature as such must perish." This is throughout a mixing up of the divine כבד and the divine קדש, whilst the fact of the words being two, points out the twofold nature of the idea. It is also a very serious misconstruction of the ethic spirit[3] of the Old Testa-

---

[1] xl. 25, lii. 10, lvii. 15, lxiii. 10 f.
[2] Theologie des A. T., 1878, p. 517.
[3] Which has lately been defended by Budde (Die Biblische Urgeschichte, 1883, pp. 65-70) with regard to another question.

ment, according to which the creature was in God's eyes "very good" (Gen. i. 31), and became displeasing only through the disobedience of man. But if, according to the Old Testament, the heart of man is evil from his youth (Gen. viii. 21), in what passage of the Old Testament is Jahveh's anger expressed against (apparently?) blameless beings unless that anger were a result of His hatred of sin committed by the beings in question? In 1 Sam. vi. 19 f., the passage quoted by Kuenen? The objection raised by Thenius,[1] that the guilt of the people of Bethshemesh was not comprehensible, has been correctly refuted by Wellhausen;[2] and that the holiness of God, as announced by the seraphim, admits only of the foregoing interpretation, is proved by Job iv. 18: "Behold, He put no trust in His servants, and His angels He charged with folly."

The same confounding of Jahveh's holiness with His excellence is now found among the evolutionists.[3] This false conception of Old Testament holiness has found particularly marked expression and significant influence with Ritschl[4] when he describes the holiness

---

[1] Die Bücher Samuelis erklärt, 2nd ed. 1864, z. St.
[2] Der Text der Bücher Samuelis, 1871, p. 65 f.
[3] For instance Kuenen, De Godsdienst, i. pp. 233-237 f.; Duhm, Theologie der Propheten, p. 169 ff.
[4] Die Christliche Lehre von der Rechtfertigung und Versöhnung,

of Jahveh, firstly, as His might and greatness; secondly, as His unapproachableness; thirdly, as His zeal in the preservation of His secrecy;[1] fourthly, as His hatred to impurity. Now, that Ritschl's interpretation of the passages in the Books of Samuel quoted by him is opposed to the pure moral tendency of the entire Old Testament has already been shown But that his fourth interpretation of holiness must lead to an under-estimate of the religious and moral historical elevation of the Old Testament, lies in the fact that he takes the "impurity" of the Old Testament to mean that which is "common and unclean," whereas it really signifies religious and moral impurity.[2]

1882, p. 90 f. Stade, Geschichte Israels, p. 433: "From the fact that Jahveh visited with the heaviest chastisement an injury or violation offered to His peculiar rights, we may infer that the term 'holy' did not suggest a moral quality to the minds of the old Israelites." Were this proposition, however, true, it follows that the severe punishments attached by all nations to insults offered to Majesty must not be regarded in a moral light. This idea Stade further enlarges upon (p. 435), when he describes this attributing of human infatuation to the God of Israel. We must, however, remember that the power or virtue of God has always been regarded in the light of rewarding to sin its appropriate consequences.

[1] 1 Sam. vi. 19 f., 2 Sam. vi. 6 f., are quoted by him.

[2] Compare my article "Reinigungen," in the Protestant. Realencyclopädie, 2nd ed. xii. (1883) p. 625.

CHAPTER X.

Was pre-prophetic Jahvism conscious that Jahveh, manifesting Himself, had entered into covenant with Israel?—Was not pre-prophetic Israel already convinced that the only God of revelation had in overflowing love chosen one from among all nations to be His first-born Son, who received a double share of the inheritance of revelation?

The answer to that question has already been given in my Offenbarungsbegriff des A. T., ii. pp. 338–40. Amos, under Jeroboam II. (about 800 B.C.), has given expression to the idea that Jahveh regarded Israel as His chosen people (iii. 2), which relationship is manifested in a special act. It is in connection with the promises and duties of the covenant that Amos says: "Therefore I will punish you for all your iniquities." The relation subsisting between Jahveh and Israel is then to be determined by certain conditions whose neglect must be detrimental to our understanding of the subject. What are we entitled to regard in the light of a covenant if such an expression as this used by Amos had not been uttered ? Hosea (vi. 7, viii. 8) describes this relationship between Israel and Jahveh by the word ברית. If the other prophets (Joel, Isaiah, Micah, Nahum) before Jeremiah have not used this word, it cannot, however, be said to be so in the case of his contemporaries (Zeph. and Habak.), or even of those succeeding (Zech. and Haggai).[1] Nor have the prophets coming immediately after Amos and Hosea regarded themselves as having imparted something new to the people, because they spoke of the all-powerful relationship between Jahveh and His people, and regarded the transaction as resting on the freewill of Jahveh and on the fulfilment of the covenant conditions. Hosea compares this relationship simply with a marriage; and who is ignorant of the fact that, according to the Jewish idea of right, this was a free transaction which could readily be annulled? (Deut. xxiv. 1). Moreover, even in Hosea it was a favourite representation setting forth the Jewish nation as the Son of God, *i.e.* to be understood as an adopted son. And does not every act of adoption imply relationship

---

[1] Such proofs have been collected by Guthe in his De fœderis notione Jeremiana (1877), p. 10 f.

resting on a free decision? (Comp. Hos. xi. 1; "When Israel was a child, then I loved him and called my Son out of Egypt.") So speaks the prophet, in entire agreement with the national consciousness that Jahveh had once, and that at the commencement of Israel's national existence, given it an all-convincing proof of His love, in that He delivered His adopted children from Egypt. This is confirmed by Isaiah (i. 2: "I have nourished and brought up children, but they have rebelled against me"). This is in agreement with what we find in Ex. iv. 22, xxix. 5 f., xxiv. 7 f.

Accordingly, Guthe, *e.g.*, is right in his conclusion (ibid. 1877, p. 10), where he says: "Quum fœderis notione usus est Jeremias ad religionem israelitaeam describendam, minime hanc rationem tanquam novam invenit." Wellhausen,[1] however, has asserted that the representation of the covenant does not occur before the time of Amos (iii. 2). It was brought out by Hosea first of all, who represented the relationship between Jahveh and Israel as one of marriage (i.–iii.). He uses the term ברית (vi. 7) only for the purposes of

---

[1] Geschichte des Volkes Israels, i. (1878); Prolegomena zur Geschichte Israels, p. 443. Comp. Stade in Theolog. Literaturzeitung (1882), No. 11.

comparison, while in viii. 1 the same term either signifies a law laid down, or the passage must be regarded as an interpolation. As to this, however, enough has already been said. In opposition to the assertion that berith first signified law and then covenant, we agree with Gesenius that its signification is (1) fœdus; (2) conditio fœderis; (3) interpres fœderis; (4) signum fœderis. This idea is supported by the following analogy. In that case פֶּה, "mouth," might also signify "command;"[1] but if פֶּה had just meant "command," it could never have come to signify "mouth." We must also regard as unfounded the opinion expressed[2] by Mühlau-Volck in the ninth edition of Gesenius' Handwörterbuch (1883), that berith could not have meant "covenant," because then the derived signification "command or ordinance" must be explained as "one-sided condition of covenant," or "one-sided alliance," and therefore a contradictio in adjecto. Friedrich Delitzsch[3] has also recently approved and defended the assertion of Mühlau-Volck in the eighth and ninth editions of Gesenius' Handwörterbuch (1878, 1883),

[1] Compare Num. xx. 24.
[2] Without taking into account our exposition of 1882.
[3] The Hebrew Language viewed in the Light of Assyrian Research (1883), p. 49.

by which berith had first the signification "ordinance," and then that of "covenant." Against that we must urge the following objections: It has long been known that the verb ברה signified "to cut, to separate, to decide." The point in question is the substantive ברית, and the question is, whether that first denoted "covenant" or first meant "decision, determination"? Now we maintain, as already stated, that "decision, ordinance," cannot have been derived from "covenant;" for if that had been the development of the significations, why should not every other Hebrew word which denoted "determination" or something similar, also have come to mean "covenant"? So berith must first have meant "covenant," and we maintain[1] that that signification is derived directly from the fundamental meaning of the verb barah, because it was usual to slaughter sacrificial animals at the making of a treaty. We see that that ceremony had, in the ancient manner of expression, karath berith, "to cut a covenant," taken a distinct character.

Was pre-prophetic Jahvism further without the

---

[1] We must rather say, as we now see, that we return to the etymology which Gesenius gave in Thesaurus Linguæ Hebraicæ, p. 237 (1829): "ברית fœdus, ab hostiis dissectis dictum."

thought that Israel was a kingdom of Jahveh, which He governed by means of extraordinary and ordinary instruments,[1] and by the Torah, which controlled partly the general conduct of Israel, and which partly affected the decision of isolated cases? Hosea says (viii. 4): "They have set up kings, but not by me: they have made princes, and I knew it not;" and again (x. 3): "Now shall they say, We have no king, because we feared not the Lord; and what then should a king do to us?" Finally (xiii. 10, 11): "Where is thy king that may save thee in all thy cities? and thy judges of whom thou saidst, Give me a king and princes? I gave thee a king in mine anger, and took him away in my wrath." We have here the prophetic view that, as Jahveh had been hitherto Israel's only king, so should He continue to be for all time. Vatke (ibid. 478, Anm.), Wellhausen (Gesch. Israels, i. p. 433 f.), along with Stade (Gesch. Israels, p. 177), regard this judgment of Hosea as something personal and irregular, which came to him through his experience of the godless monarchs of his day. We are, however, convinced that we cannot lay too much stress on the passages quoted, although those passages must be combined with the fourth verse of chapter iii. For

[1] Prophets, heroes, and priests.

the expressions[1] used by the prophet (xiii. 10) point too plainly to the Israelites' petition for a king[2] to be taken for anything else than an intentional allusion of the speaker to the national tradition. Therefore we must abide by the decision that Hosea (in xiii. 10) is looking back upon the institution of the earthly kingdom, and that he (iii. 5) mentions the kingdom of David only as the comparatively God-pleasing part of that kingdom.[3]

From these portions of Hosea we see that Israel, in the desire for earthly kings, departed from its original relationship to Jahveh. We must, however, recognise it as a Mosaic idea (comp. Ex. xix. 5, 6) that Israel should become a kingdom of priests. For example, Deut. xxxiii. 5 regards neither Moses nor Saul, but Jahveh, as the King reigning over Israel in the law of Moses. This ancient but yet correct view of the relationship subsisting between the kingdom of Israel and the kingdom of Jahveh is further illustrated in

[1] Thou Israel hast said: "Give me a king and princes."
[2] 1 Sam. viii. 6: "Give us a king to judge us."
[3] We have found an ally in Bertheau, who, in opposition to Wellhausen, decidedly proves in his Commentar zum Buch der Richter und Ruth the song of Deborah to be a literary testimony, in which the consciousness that "Jahveh is the ruler of Israel, appears in the strongest light, that He encourages His people to war, that He enters into the midst of the fight, and that He reveals Himself to His enemies as the representative of the rights of Israel."

Gideon's decision (Judg. viii. 23). This is shown in its historical light in the parable uttered by Jotham (Judg. ix. 7–20), where the nobler men, having first refused to assume the regal position, the inferior Abimelech has accepted it. Accordingly, we conclude that the representations of the choice of Saul correspond with those set forth by Moses, which regard the choosing of Saul as a rejection of Jahveh (1 Sam. viii., x. 17–27, xi., xii.). It is not to be wondered at that Samuel and the later prophets struggled against the violent and sinful tendencies of their age, which regarded Israel as an earthly kingdom apart from God. Stade furnishes no proof as to the original leanings of Moses and the prophets when he says (ibid. p. 177): "In Judah, Hosea's opinion concerning the kingdom was not in existence prior to the exile." He is not able to prove the statement made in p. 176, that the unsettled nature of their earthly kingdom was but a result of Israel's political condition after the exile. For has not the Elohist (whose conception at the time of the captivity Stade accepts, ibid. p. 62 f., but which he does not mention in the discussion of the question on hand) regarded Abraham as the forefather of the kings? (Gen. xvii. 6, xvi. 20, etc.). Has the historian rejected Saul and his successors on the throne? Has he not even mentioned the touching instance of loyalty shown to Saul by the men of Jabesh? (1 Chron x. 11, 12). Has he not blamed Saul on account of his disobedience to Jahveh by whom he was chosen king? (vers. 11, 12). Has he not extolled David and all the kings faithful to Jahveh? Also in our controversy with Wellhausen and Stade regarding the disputed derivation of the word "Torah," we were not without supporters, for the etymology of the word תורה, assumed by Gesenius and (1882) justified by us in detail, has also been defended, notwithstanding Wellhausen and Stade,[1]

---

[1] Wellhausen (Gesch. Israels, i. p. 410) and Stade (Theolog. Literaturzeitung, 1882, No. 11) had stated that "תּוֹרָה comes from הִפִּיל גּוֹרָל = הוֹרָה (to cast a lot), and signifies the decision by lot given by the מוֹרֶה (teacher, instructor), especially the כֹּהֵן, the كاٰدِن (soothsayer)." In favour of such an assertion, however, we can find no proof, for in the references גִּבְעַת מוֹרֶה, אֵלוֹן מוֹרֶה (Judg. vii.; Gen. xii. 6), moreh can have attached to it the general signification of "teacher" or "instructor," and does not require to be regarded as meaning "prophet" or "oracle." Against that idea, however, there are two reasons which demand attention. First, the term הוֹרָה never occurs again with the object גּוֹרָל, still the reasons are not sufficient for us to sever this connection. Secondly, it would be somewhat hazardous to assert that such a word as goral (lot) should be allowed to disappear from a language. Much more must be accepted to warrant that so general a word as jad (hand) could be dissociated from הוֹרָה, to throw. (Comp. my Historisch-kritisches Lehrgebäude der Hebr. Sprache, i. (1881) p. 286.)

by Mühlau-Volck and Ryssel.[1] So the expression "Torah" is not derived from the casting of lots by the priests in Israel.

We have described in the Offenbarungsbegriff des A. T., ii. p. 345, the service performed by the priests as narrated in the Old Testament. In the Old Testament the priests are certainly brought into connection with the law (Hos. iv. 6, etc.); but the priests had only to preserve the law, and to hand it down from generation to generation. It belonged to them, moreover, to interpret it, but it was beyond their province to produce a law. This view is corroborated by such a passage as Mal. ii. 7 : "For the priest's lips should keep knowledge, and they should seek the law at his mouth : for he is the messenger of the Lord of hosts." Accordingly, the answers given by God through the high priest must be regarded in the light of responses given to certain inquiries. With regard to the remaining conditions of the covenant, the priests had only to apply[2] the use of the secondary instruments appointed by the God of revelation, and to ascertain His will in the matter of peculiar cases by the use of outward

---

[1] The former in the ninth edition of Gesenius' Handwörterbuch (1883), *s.v.* ; the latter in his review of Bredenkamp's Gesetz und Propheten in the Göttingische Gelehrte Anzeigen (1883), p. 683.

[2] That is, to preserve, to use, to detail.

means, viz. the sacred lot. In the tendency (aims?) of Old Testament theology as examined by us in the above-named work, too little is seldom, too much is often, attributed to the priests.

Stade[1] commits the former error when he says: "No one except the prophets found any fault with the national cultus." Such assertions as that are made, and yet in Hos. iv. 6 the priests are called the mouthpieces of the law![2] The priests were also the allies of the prophets in their relation to the apostate people. The frequent friendships between the prophets and the priests confirm this view (comp. Isa. viii. 2, etc.). Consequently, we have no right to doubt what is told us in 2 Kings xii. 3 of the high priest Jehoiada; and Merx[3] observes correctly that Bamoth were removed more through priestly, than prophetic, influence. Duhm[4] also places the high priest Hilkiah at the head of the party of prophets that emanated from Isaiah.

The second mistake is committed by Kuenen, for in his latest book[5] he gives to priestly efficacy a greater

---

[1] Zeitschrift für die alttestl. Wissenschaft (1883), p. 9.
[2] Compare the excellent remarks of Nowack on this subject in Der Prophet Hosea erklärt (1880), p. 30.
[3] The Prophecy of Joel and its Exponents from the Earliest Times to the Reformers (1879), p. 7.
[4] Theologie der Propheten (1875), p. 196.
[5] Volksreligion u. Weltreligion, pp. 81-87, 96.

fundamental significance than belongs to it by right. According to his exposition, the name Kôhen represents the priest as a person who could reveal mysteries—a soothsayer or an augur. Further, he describes the instructive and magisterial functions of the priests, not as a means of making known the moral fundamental principles of the religion of Jahveh and His will regarding isolated cases, but as an agency which had created these moral principles and maxims of justice. In short, from Kuenen's point of view it would appear as if, in the earlier period of the religious history of Israel, the priests were the only instruments of Jahveh until towards the end of the time of the Judges. The Nabiismus had gone over [1] from the Canaanites to the Israelites, and Samuel became priest and prophet, and was thus the originator of the prophetism of Israel.

Further, the opinion (also formerly defended by Kuenen [2]) as to the rank denoted by the word Kôhen [3] is wrong, for the word in question signifies only the preparer or servant κατ' ἐξοχήν, that is to say, the person who has charge of the most important department of

[1] For a contradiction of that last assertion, see Offenbarungsbegriff des A. T., i. pp. 63-69.

[2] De Godsdienst, i. p. 210.

[3] For the sense and importance of this double signification of the vowel-lengths, see my Historisch-kritisches Lehrgebäude der Hebr. Sprache, i. p. 28.

human service—the worship of the Deity.¹ We can only express ourselves as Hoffmann² does when he says: "*The Arabs ascribed soft murmuring to their Kâhĭn.*" Then, with regard to the creative power of the priesthood, it would appear from Kuenen as if the Jahvism represented by the priests were a power independent of preceding or contemporaneous prophetic activity. One should not, however, attempt to place on an equality priests and prophets in their relation to Old Testament religion. It must not be forgotten that, according to Israelitish tradition, Moses was a prophet, but Aaron a priest; that since the departure from Egypt Jahveh did not cease to send prophets to His people (Jer. vii. 25), and that the priests submitted themselves to those prophets as agents superior³ to themselves.⁴

In Old Testament researches, such bold speculative theories as the following from Duhm's Theologie der Proph., p. 199, should not gain currency: "It would

[1] Compare Gesenius in Thesaurus Linguæ Hebr., p. 661 f., with Fleischer in Delitzsch, Jesaja, at lxi. 10; compare also for the etymology of Nabi, as the speaker κατ' ἐξοχήν, my detailed exposition in the Offenbarungsbegriff des A. T., i. pp. 71-76.

[2] Zeitschrift für die alttestl. Wissenschaft, 1883, p. 88.

[3] Because extraordinary and direct.

[4] If such undoubted facts may be thrust aside, then it is easy for Lippert to include the Old Testament religion in his Geschichte des Priesterthums, vol. ii. (1884) p. 11 ff.; compare principally p. 531.

seem as if the tribe of Levi, from which Moses sprang, had been animated by a spirit similar to that which retained the Rechabites in their nomadic life, and which produced the Nasiräismus and the older prophetism." The most ancient history of priesthood cannot be so far detached from its traditions regarding Aaron, Eleazar, Phinehas, and the high priest at Shiloh. Vatke shows a true perception of the real relation between priesthood and prophetism (ibid. p. 226, note), and Merx correctly remarks (Die Prophetie des Joel, 1879, p. 34): "In later times the alliance was formed which did not exist in its original nature between prophetism and priesthood." The correct view is also adopted by Riehm in his Handwörterbuch des Biblischen Alterthums, article "Priests," p. 1225.

We are, however, led to further examination by the following remark: It has been pointed out,[1] as an important fact in the development of Israelitish religion, that the will of God was first made known by writing in Deuteronomy. But firstly,—and that is the chief point in question,—it is not possible that the substance and nature of a national religion could

[1] Comp. Smend, Die Genesis des Judenthums, pp. 95, 134, and also Reville, Prolegomènes de l'histoire des religions, Paris 1881, p. 197. The latter in his derivation of priestly authority regards the priests too much on the same level with the prophets.

be changed because the dogmatic moral principles of religious life were no longer expressed orally, but by writing; secondly, it must also be maintained that the fundamental rules and basis of the Israelitish religion had already been laid down by Moses in the decalogue.

CHAPTER XI.

The legal basis possessed by pre-prophetic Jahvism.—With regard to the lex cærimonalis, or the places, persons, rites, and times consecrated to religion, we abide, on the one hand, by the negative [1] judgment that, in the consideration of these things parallel with the progressive revelation of God, new structures were set up on the old foundations. But, on the other hand, we are of the positive opinion [2] that the fundamental basis of Israel's religious conduct had already been laid down in the youth (Hos. xi. 1) or the time of the espousals of that nation (Jer. iii. 4). In confirmation of this, we add the following: Von Orelli [3] was of the opinion that if the Mosaic authority of the religious ordinances of the prophecies (Jer. vii. 22 f., etc.) could be called in question, it might also be denied that Moses had written the decalogue, for Isaiah (chap.

---

[1] Offenbarungsbegriff des A. T., ii. pp. 321-332.
[2] Ibid. ii. pp. 333-336, 346 f., 348 f., 351.
[3] Article "Israel" in the Protestant. Realencyclopädie, vii. (1880) p. 172.

i. 10) speaks lightly of the Sabbath (ver. 13), and therefore could not have regarded it as a Mosaic institution. Nevertheless Orelli should have pointed out the fact that Isaiah describes the stretching forth of unclean hands in prayer to God as displeasing[1] to Him (ver. 15), and that the things enumerated in vers. 11–16 are meant as religious ordinances originating with God in a different sense and degree. The following circumstance proves it: The words, "I cannot away with" (ver. 13), are applied to the Sabbath from a material reason; but the words, "Who hath required this?" of the 12th verse do not refer to the Sabbath. So a careful exegesis of Isa. i. 10–17 shows that, because the prophet mentions the Sabbath (ver. 13), he did not consider the Decem Verba as un-Mosaic. To assert that this passage of Isaiah denies the Mosaic authority of the decalogue would be as incorrect an exposition[2] of it as to say that it does not contain a denial of the Mosaic origin of the religious ordinances of the Pentateuch annexed to the decalogue.

Secondly, it must be regarded as inconsistent with the authority of Israelitish tradition, and utterly

---

[1] Although this stretching forth of hands took its rise from general revelation, in the involuntary striving of the body together with the soul towards the unseen, and not in the source of special revelation.

[2] Also of Amos v. 25; Jer. vii. 22 f., etc. etc.

impossible, that the paschal feast should have assumed its historical significance without historical grounds.¹ It cannot be doubted that the death of the first-born in Egypt, or at least of the king's son, was a fact, because it is a supposition which has a bearing on the whole existence of Israel. Then Pesach, although it originally meant the transition of the sun into the sign of Aries,² might yet have rightly assumed the new signification of the passing over of the destroying angel. Further, Wellhausen's³ explanation of the Massoth from the course of nature seems to me impossible. For why should not a half or a whole day have been allowed for the leavening of the dough, or why should the thanksgiving for the first-fruits of the barley-harvest not have been postponed for the same length of time ? Wellhausen's explanation of the unleavened bread is therefore an untenable supposition. There must rather have been some historical reason for the institution of the unleavened bread. That ground

---

¹ Compare the disputed opinion with George's Die älteren jüdischen Feste (1835), pp. 151, 153, 172 ; but principally with Wellhausen's Geschichte Israels, p. 85 f. ; Prolegomena, p. 85 f.

² The view even of Von Lengerke in his Kenaan, p. 381.

³ Geschichte Israels, p. 88 ; Prolegomena, p. 89 : "They did not leave the first-fruits of the harvest-time to be leavened, kneaded, and baked, but quickly made a kind of pot-cake of it ; that was the true Massoth."

was the traditional and sufficiently important fact that the dismissal of the Israelites from Egypt, so long refused them, was finally granted with such precipitation that not even the partially fermented dough could remain in the kneading troughs. But as Israel retained[1] the natural signification of the three feasts of assembly, and worshipped Jahveh also in later times as the giver of the blessings of nature, it is difficult to understand how these feasts should have assumed a traditional significance if the history of the nation had not furnished a reason for it. If national tradition had not given a historical meaning to the feasts, Israel would then have had to be content with praising Jahveh as the giver of the blessings which accrued to it in the natural course of the year.

Thirdly, in entering on the subject of the ceremonial and moral law, we are met by a point, concerning which I must oppose the evolution theory that has recently been advanced. Duhm[2] maintains that "the author of Deuteronomy believed that he could impress, outwardly at least, the stamp of holiness upon the Israelites, and through such a stamp distinguish them from the heathen nations." But the author of

[1] Which was not superseded by the historical meaning.
[2] Theologie der Propheten, p. 197 f.

Deuteronomy, that lawgiver of Israel who has most strongly emphasized the inward motive-power of the fulfilling[1] of the law, cannot be accused of having introduced "external religion" into Israel. Secondly, Isaiah, from whom, according to Duhm, the author of Deuteronomy materially borrowed the ideal of holiness, originated[2] no new idea of holiness in Israel. As Duhm's notion of holiness is connected with that of purity, it may be added that the conception of purity has also been proved to be pre-Isaiahic, for it is already mentioned[3] by Hosea (ix. 3) as a majesty requiring no further explanation. Kuenen,[4] however, has misapprehended the true history of the religious æsthetic purity of Israel even more than Duhm. For as that purity appears in the prophecies as an understood feature of an Israelite united to Jahveh, as it appears in Deuteronomy[5] in almost all its aspects, finally, as it rested on the fear of death or on all that suggested death,[6] so Kuenen is wrong in his conception of purity

---

[1] Grateful love to Jahveh, the God of salvation.
[2] Compare the foregoing proof on p. 81 f.
[3] Compare, further, my article "Reinigungen," in the Protestantischen Realencyclopädie, xii. (1883) pp. 618-617 ; also p. 627.
[4] Volksreligion u. Weltreligion, pp. 83 f., 150, 160 f.
[5] Which is, according to Kuenen, the fruit of the prophetism of that time.
[6] Compare the proof in PRE², xii. 618 ff.

when he says that "it displays the character of the claims of Jahveh according to the priestly notion of them, and contains an emblematic representation of morality."

Fourthly, it is an unhistorical assertion[1] that it was a peculiarity of the prophets to emphasize exclusively the moral character of religion.

(*a*) That salvation depended on the religious moral bent of mankind was known before the time of the writing prophets. Religion and morality were from the beginning the basis of Israel's favour[2] with God, while the old covenant conditions (Gen. xvii. 1; Ex. xix. 5, etc.) are a reflection of this consciousness on the part of ancient Israel, and we have no historical ground for the assertion[3] that it was the prophets who first "placed the righteous God and His sinful people in opposition to each other." On the contrary, Moses, Samuel, Nathan, Ahijah, Elijah, etc., knew and announced this fact in its full severity. Therefore it would be a violent interpretation of Scripture to institute an antithesis between

---

[1] Smend in Die Genesis des Judenthums, p. 131.

[2] That is shown by the mere existence of such narratives as those of Cain, Achan, the sons of Eli, etc., which display the moral views of Israel. The sons of Eli held priestly offices, yet that did not prevent them from losing the favour of God through their immorality.

[3] Smend in Die Genesis des Judenthums, p. 128.

Ancient Israel's Religion. 169

the so-called active prophets and those prophets of the more literary period of Israel's history, with regard to the theory of the importance and saving influence of morality, whilst the practical application of the theory may, in the course of centuries, have been more forcibly insisted upon by Jahveh's agents, because Israel's capability to transgress and its load of guilt had increased.

(b) Neither was it the writing prophets who lent to religion its exclusively moral character. According to them, Israel's covenant with the God of revelation rested rather on a dogmatic-metaphysical foundation, on the positive exercise of Jahveh's influence on the history of that nation (Hos. xi. 1,[1] etc.). If, too, according to the writing prophets, the hope of salvation, the unbrokenness of covenant union with God, the well-being[2] (צדקה) of the Israelites, depended on their moral bent and their inclination to fulfil the ethic terms of Jahveh's covenant; if the older writing prophets disputed the Mosaic authority, and consequently the divine origin, of the ordinances of worship, as well as their direct connection with

[1] The gracious condescension to immanency on the part of the transcendent God.

[2] Kautzsch in his programme, Ueber die Derivate des Stammes צרק im alttestamentlichen Sprachgebrauch (1881), p. 53.

special revelation,—nevertheless cultus [1] was regarded by them as an emblem of Israel's fidelity to Jahveh, an emblem involuntarily created in the heart of man, originating in Israel's national union, and therefore belonging to human religion and general revelation, and estimated according to its relative worth.[2]

(c) Neither did the prophets of the seventh century think [3] differently from those of the eighth regarding "the cancelling of sin." For Jeremiah [4] also mentions the existence of priestly Levites in the future following the day of judgment (Jer. xxxiii. 17-26), and Ezekiel's view (xxxvi. 26) teaches much of the spirituality of the bond between Israel and Jahveh, and agrees with that of Jeremiah (xxxi. 31-34) regarding the future activity of persons consecrated to religion, and even the bringing of sin-offerings (Ezek. xliii. 19). Now, if Deutero-Isaiah's spiritual view of fasting (lviii. 6) is compared with his prophecy

---

[1] With its four departments of service: place, persons, actions (rites?), and time.

[2] Compare Isaiah's promises concerning the temple (iv. 5 f., xxx. 19, xxxi. 5 f.), his friendship for the priest Uriah (viii. 2), and his words relating to "the song and the gladness of heart in the night of holy solemnity" (xxx. 29).

[3] In Smend's opinion (Die Genesis des Judenthums, p. 128), Duhm has shown that difference.

[4] Duhm himself (Die Theologie der Propheten, p. 215) must admit that.

that after his time the Israel of the happy future should bring to the house of Jahveh offerings in a clean vessel (Isa. lxvi. 20), and if Malachi's zeal for faultless burnt-offerings (i. 14) is compared with his denunciation of immorality (iii. 5), it will be more easily acknowledged that Israel's religious principles have always been in theory essentially the same, that is to say, covenant faith and covenant obedience.[1] Whether the latter implies obedience principally to the moral law, or indirect observance of the ceremonial law, are unessentially different aspects of the same matter.

[1] For instance, Gen. xv. 6 ; Ex. xx. 2 f.; Isa. vii. 9 ; Hab. ii. 4.

CHAPTER XII.

Did pre-prophetic Jahvism miss the thought (knowledge?) of the future universalism of Israel's salvation?—
The opinion that particularism suited the early religion of Israel, and that the idea of universalism was first added by the later representatives of written prophecy, is now becoming a dogma. The following is a proof of it. K. Planck[1] was so firmly convinced of the absolute particularism of the pre-prophetic religion of Israel, that he felt himself constrained to add a *national* starting-point for the Old Testament view of the universe to the *religious* one[2] already in existence. Further, Tiele believed that the religion of the Old Testament ought[3] to be classed among

---

[1] "Der Ursprung des Mosaismus," in the Tübinger Theologischen Jahrbüchern, vol. iv. (1845) pp. 450-519, 656-721; chiefly pp. 452-454.

[2] Which was, according to Planck's view, "pure fire-worship," ibid. p. 455; comp. preceding p. 46.

[3] Vergel. Geschiedenis, p. 2: "All ancient cultus have one characteristic in common which distinguishes them from newer forms

antique religions, expressly on account of its purely national limits. Kuenen also asserts in his latest work,[1] that only after the moral character of Jahveh and the doctrine of ethic monotheism had been taught by the prophets to the people, "could the latter have regarded Jahveh as something more than their conqueror." In refutation of that view, we shall not content ourselves with pointing out that Von Lengerke's[2] theory would have been more just to the true course of the Israelitish development of ideas, but will state briefly what seems to us a correct judgment of the essential features of Old Testament representations of the future.

Firstly, concerning the kind of prosperity promised in the Old Testament, we have already explained[3] that two ideas are contained in it, a preparative and a conclusive idea, the one indicating worldly, the other spiritual prosperity.

Secondly, with regard to the number of those

---

of worship: they are all primitive or national religions;" p. 6: "Although the heathen gods were as filth and nothingness compared with Jahveh, yet even the Israelites never thought of making proselytes to their religion, until other nations set them the example, and the idea of a universal religion began to ripen."

[1] Volksreligion u. Weltreligion, pp. 125-133.
[2] Kenaan (1844), pp. 489-494.
[3] Offenbarungsbegriff des A. T., ii. 396-398.

sharing in the prosperity, viz. of those persons who, in spite of the constant guilt attendant on their endeavours to please God, should yet, through repentance and faith,[1] obtain a share in the promised prosperity (or prosperity attained at the close of their religious history), we judge that Jahvism, from the beginning, possessed in principle the tendency to universal propagation, even if that quality had been a latent one in the religion of revelation. For after that Israel, in Moses' time, had become thoroughly convinced of the immense superiority of Jahveh to all other supernatural powers, after Israel had recognised its God as the Disposer of all earthly events, then it must also have felt itself superior to all other nations from a national point of view, and must have possessed the thought that its religion should yet become the universal faith. Since the pre-prophetic religion of Israel cannot be imagined without that principal and potential universalism, which it received, at the latest, while yet in infancy in the time of Moses, together with the consciousness of a supernatural source of origin, then it agrees with the true causal nexus of the history of

---

[1] Isa. vii. 3 : "A remnant shall return ;" ver. 9 : "If ye will not believe, surely ye shall not be established ; " Hab. ii. 4 : The just shall gain eternal life through that faith which is the source of his righteousness (of his covenant relationship).

religion, that the future destiny of the whole human race was interwoven with Abraham's call: "In thy seed shall all the nations of the earth be blessed" (Gen. xii. 3, xxii. 18).

But if this universal aim of Jahveh religion found expression only in the negative manner mentioned above,[1] that arose from various reasons, viz. the want of a divine command to spread that religion,[2] the hostile attitude of other nations towards Israel, and the national reserve of all the races of former times, on which account a mission was out of the question.[3] Besides, there were early Gentile adherents, and therefore proselytes of the Jahveh religion. For even the uncircumcised Gentile might rejoice before Jahveh at the sacrificial feasts, and might, according to the legal rites of reception, constitute himself, with full right,

---

[1] Comp. all the prophecies in which are threats or promises having reference to the Gentiles. All illustrate the consciousness of Israel that Jahveh was the disposer of earthly events, and would finally, through chastisement or reward, lead all men to acknowledge Him.

[2] Comp. Acts xiv. 16: "Who in times past suffered all nations to walk in their own ways." Comp. also Offenbarungsbegriff des A. T., i. p. 35.

[3] As regards the relation between the Israelitish state and the Gentiles, we think it well to quote a correct and important sentence from Riehm's Handwörterbuch (p. 448): "By no other ancient people were laws relating to strangers so liberally and humanely framed as by the Israelites, so unjustly charged with narrow-minded particularism."

one of Jahveh's chosen people.[1] It is, however, to be specially noticed that there was a difference between the political and the religious connection of a Gentile with Israel. The latter had different grades, and the relationship to Jahveh could only be attained by a special rite of reception.[2] So it is evident that Israel carried on from the beginning what was at least a home mission.

We see further that, before the time of the writing prophets, certain incidents took place, hitherto unnoticed in our researches, which gradually extended Israel's home mission into a foreign one.[3] The Queen of Sheba, who had heard of "the fame of Solomon concerning the name of the Lord," whilst admiring the wisdom and knowledge of the world of the Israelitish king, was led to perceive in Israel's God the true source of that wisdom. Elijah was prompted to benefit the widow of Zarephath, both temporally and spiritually, by his presence. We see Elisha, not only exercising

---

[1] Deut. xvi. 11; Gen. xvii. 23, xxxiv. 16: "One people;" Ex. iv. 26; Num. x. 29-32. Through these references we merely wish to render prominent certain features illustrative of Israelitish consciousness, which are interwoven with its earliest history. For the legal and prophetic passages, see Riehm's Handwörterbuch, p. 449.

[2] Amongst other nations, the political union of a foreigner with the natives did not include a religious connection, the latter having to be obtained by a special rite.

[3] 1 Kings x. 1, 9, xvii. 8-24; 2 Kings v. 17, viii. 7-15.

his miraculous power on Naaman the Syrian, and inciting him to erect the first altar to Jahveh beyond the limits of Israel, but also commissioned by his God to exert a direct and positive influence on the history of Syria. Then the mission of Jonah, the son of Amittai, as a preacher of repentance to Nineveh in the time of Jeroboam II. (about 800), might, according to religious historical supposition, have been possible, and this ideal basis of his story been brought out of its obscurity in the Book of Jonah to the broad light of day, if only a single act[1] had been recorded in tradition connected with Jonah. For how could he be conceived as the first agent of Israel's foreign mission without such an historical motive?

After such incidents as these had formed a connection between the home and the foreign mission of Israel, it became more easy to define in words[2] and to realize in facts the principle, at first latent in the religion of revelation, viz. that it should subdue the whole earth, and bring all men to their knees before the God of revelation.

[1] Perhaps a journey undertaken for some purpose and from some motive to the great town on the Tigris.
[2] Ps. viii. 1 : "O Lord, our Lord, how excellent is Thy name in all the earth! who hast set Thy glory above the heavens!" (comp. my Historisch-kritisches Lehrgebäude der Hebr. Sprache, i. p. 303 f.); also Isa. ii. 2-4 ; Micah iv. 1-3, etc.

M

The pretended particularism of the earlier religion of Israel is connected with its supposed nationalism.[1] It has been asserted that the pre-prophetic religion of Israel influenced that one nation alone, and also, that in its primary stage Old Testament religion affected only the whole nation, single individuals being lost in the mass, but in the course of the prophetic period we are told each one singly expected his salvation from God, so that Old Testament religion acquired[2] the quality of individualism.

But, in the first place, even the earliest adherents of the faith of Jahveh believed in the salvation of single individuals, and we must regard[3] the individual cry of Jacob, "I have waited for Thy salvation, O Lord" (Gen. xlix. 18), as a pious ejaculation such as ascended from every truly religious soul in ancient Israel. All the old narratives treat of the salvation or perdition of single individuals, such as Esau,

---

[1] Or "totalism," if we may be allowed to coin new words.

[2] So Smend says in his work, Ueber die Genesis des Judenthums, p. 131: "The Israelitish religion became through the prophets more than a relation between God and a nation; it was also a relation between God and the single individual. Not only the nation as a whole, but each person singly, expected his salvation from God." See further in his programme, Die Listen der Bücher Esra und Nehemiah (1881), p. 33.

[3] Even if "Jacob's blessing" in its present form was not the utterance of the patriarch.

Reuben, Joseph, etc.; and although the words, "I have brought thee out of the land of Egypt," with which the decalogue begins, are applied to the whole nation, yet the command, "Honour thy father," must have been intended for each one singly. Also from the beginning, offerings were brought in Israel, not by the nation only, but by single individuals, as, for example, by Elkanah (1 Sam. i. 3). Observe, too, the individual nature of Nathan's prophecy.[1] Secondly, if the prophets had changed the totalism of Old Testament religion by "exclusively emphasizing[2] its moral character," yet between the altered manner of applying salvation and its relation to the single individual, no logical connection exists. So that no new theory was started by the writing prophets regarding the important elements of Israel's religion.[3] Finally, it must at least be admitted that the moral teaching and spiritualizing of the Israelitish religion, which, it is asserted, appears exclusively in the middle writing prophets, disappeared in the latest section of written prophecy,[4] and that there-

[1] 2 Sam. vii. 14, and this primitive root of David-Messianic prophecy proves its historical truth, whilst it is the source not only of David's last words (2 Sam. xxiii. 2), but also of the 2nd, 72nd, 89th Psalms, and perhaps of the 110th.
[2] According to Smend, Genesis des Judenthums, p. 131.
[3] Comp. the proof on preaching, p. 168 f.
[4] Comp. Duhm's Theologie der Propheten, p. 264 f.

fore the spiritualizing of Israel's religion could no longer have been existing as a cause when its effect, the subjectivizing and individualizing of religion, is said to have begun.

Thirdly, the asserted individualizing and subjectivizing of the religion of Israel was not effected either in or after the prophetic period. For the only pious person in the community which returned from exile, knew himself to be one of the chosen people, and traced his relation to Jahveh from his genealogical relation to Israel.[1] The universalism of the prophets does not mean a levelling of the differences existing between Israel and other nations, but a joining of the other nations to Israel,[2] and the Israel of the time after the captivity only hoped and strove for the universality of the true religion, in order that the Gentiles might be received into the national union.

[1] Comp. Ezra ii. 62; Neh. xiii. 26 ff.; Job i. 1; Josephi Vita, § 1 (αἱ δημόσιαι δίλτοι); Luke ii. 36.

[2] To the above refutations of Kuenen's theories (Volksreligion u. Weltreligion, p. 126) we must add the following remarks: Although Jahveh might be, according to the idea of a prophet, something more than the destroyer of strange nations, it does not follow as a natural consequence that the creed of that prophet must be less a national and more a universal religion than that of the Old Testament. For a prophet, in announcing his God as something more than the annihilator of foreign nations, may yet abide firmly by his particularism if he means that the Gentiles should be incorporated with the chosen people.

Kuenen, on the other hand, has confounded in his Darstellung[1] the two ideas of "a religion with a tendency to subjugate," and "a religion indifferent towards distinguishing national marks of relationship."

Kuenen[2] concluded, from the newness of the covenant promised by Jeremiah, that "in truth this covenant must have been independent of the relationship in which Jahveh had stood to His people since their departure from Egypt, that it was a new covenant, and therefore not limited to one nation, but adapted to and intended for all people." Yet in Jeremiah's prophecy the words, "I will make a new covenant with the house of Israel and with the house of Judah," express the fundamental determination, and it can only be inferred from them that each one was to bear the law of God in his heart. And where is it said that the covenant made by Jahveh with the re-united portions of His chosen people was intended for all nations? Is it to be assumed from the words of Jeremiah that he did not presuppose circumcision to be the reception rite for such Gentiles as wished to join themselves to the chosen people? Neither the prophetic nor the post-prophetic literature of Israel gives us the right to

---

[1] Volksreligion u. Weltreligion, pp. 125-147, 173-185.
[2] Ibid. p. 146; Jer. xxxi. 31-34.

answer that question in the affirmative.[1] We might rather say that the universal nature of late Hebrew literature has its direct fruit in the proselytizing tendencies of the scribes, and in Peter's shrinking from a mission to the Gentiles. It was special announcements alone, from the God of revelation, that led to the resolution taken at the apostles' meeting, by which the obstacles to the universal aims of the gospel of Jesus were torn down.[2] So, when the assertion that the Israelitish religion first received the characteristic of individualism[3] from the writing prophets (and from Jeremiah in particular) falls to the ground for want of Old Testament support, it can no longer be inferred that Israel had been a nation before the captivity, but after it a religious sect.[4] This supposition is connected in the minds of those who entertain it with the idea that, before the captivity, the fellowship of the Jahveh-worshippers had been founded on their natural union as a people inhabiting the same country, but that after their return from exile, the basis of their communion

---

[1] For besides the circumcision of the heart, Jeremiah (iv. 4, ix. 26) meant that of the body.

[2] Comp. Zech. viii. 20-23 ; Matt. xxiii. 15 ; Acts x. 14 ff., xv. 7 ff.

[3] That expression is also used by Kuenen in Volksreligion und Weltreligion, p. 145.

[4] Smend, Die Genesis des Judenthums, p. 139 ; Wellhausen, Geschichte Israels, pp. 1, 428 f. ; Prolegomena, pp. 1, 446.

had been the primary elements of fellowship with God,[1] viz. interest for what was spiritual and religious contemplation. The facts of the case are, that although Israel's national independence disappeared more rapidly after the captivity than previous to it, still it remained as before a nation and a religious community.

[1] Comp. Smend, Die Genesis des Judenthums, p. 139 : "Before the captivity Israel had felt itself to be a young vigorous nation, in complete harmony with its God, and protected by Him, etc. Ancient Israel had the will of Jahveh embodied in its priests and prophets, and therefore in itself;" p. 119 : "Israel's consciousness of appertainment to God accorded completely with its consciousness as a nation. Jahveh became Israel's God when Israel first came into existence;" p. 121 : "Generally speaking, there was no clear idea of the difference between Jahveh's will regarding the public conscience and the public life."

CHAPTER XIII.

Was pre-prophetic Jahvism wanting in the formal dignity of prophetic religion, that is to say, of the prophetic basis?—The defenders of the Old Testament criticism examined by us in the present work certainly do not seem to have placed[1] Israel's prophetism in the correct relation to the ordinarily transcendental world, and in the writings of these scholars we find utterances according to which the pre-prophetic religion of Israel was far more a natural production of that people.

Now, the assertion that the Jahvism of ancient Israel was a natural production, and as a national

[1] It is not our intention to return to that question in the present work. We will only add that earnest investigation of religious history can never be satisfied by such theories as those of Vatke, p. 533; of Smend in his Genesis des Judenthums, pp. 124, 129, 131, 138; and of Kuenen in his Volksreligion und Weltreligion, p. 148. For the true relation between history and prophecy, compare rather our Offenbarungsbegriff des A. T., ii. pp. 278-318. Even in Vatke (p. 148) and Smend (pp. 125-134) we get a glimpse of the correct picture of Israelitish prophetism through their self-contradiction.

religion[1] one which found utterance through the priests, we have already refuted. It only remains to be pointed out that a correct investigation of Old Testament theology would not look[2] for the representatives of the genuine religion of Israel amongst those prophets whom the people called "their wise and prudent" (Isa. xxix. 14), but whom Isaiah (v. 21) described in these words: "Woe to them that are wise in their own eyes and prudent in their own eyesight," and whom the pious of Israel, the faithful of Jahveh, the supporters of Israel's high genuine religious principles and spirituality, acknowledged neither as heroes of the great past nor as patrons of the true religion of their nation.

Secondly, it does not follow that the pre-prophetic cultus of Israel was a natural production because it agreed with the Canaanitish worship in the religious distinction of certain mountains, trees, and stones, for it has already been proved[3] that these accidental elements of the ancient Israelitish religion had nothing to do with its conception of God.

---

[1] Smend, Die Genesis des Judenthums, pp. 118, 119.

[2] Which Smend and Kuenen have done, the former in Die Genesis des Judenthums, p. 95 ; the latter in Volksreligion u. Weltreligion, pp. 93-99.

[3] Compare preceding p. 128, note 1.

But, thirdly, must not ancient Israel's conception of God have grown mechanically out of the national temperament, since it corresponded with the conception of Jahveh formed by the neighbouring races? This was not only Ghillany's[1] but also Kuenen's[2] idea. Nevertheless, we have already proved that it would be robbing Old Testament theology of its peculiar spirit and pith to expunge the uniqueness which belongs to ancient Israelitish views of the Deity, and to place the conception of God formed by Moses, Deborah, or Samuel, on a level with that of a Canaanite or a Moabite.

Fourthly, Smend has emphasized an element of history which has not been mentioned in the preceding researches, and which seems to speak with the weight of a historical fact for the inferiority of the formal dignity of the pre-prophetic worship of Israel. It is the circumstance that the Ten Tribes were not restored through their religion.[3] Is, then, the naturalness of ancient Israel's religious principle the consequence of its more limited influence on earlier history? But even if that lesser influence

---

[1] In the paragraph: "The relation of Jahveh to the gods of the neighbouring nations," pp. 429-489.

[2] De Godsdienst, i. p. 223 ff.

[3] Smend, Die Genesis Judenthums, chiefly p. 117.

were explained by the fact that Israel had at first stronger temptations to overcome, yet it proves nothing for the inferiority of old Israelitish religious principle. Further, who can doubt, when it is a question of explaining the remaining in exile of the Ten Tribes, that in the kingdoms of Israel and Judah the same religious principle existed independently of the natural tendencies of the national mind? In order to make that fact intelligible, we only need to consider that the opportunity of return did not offer itself so soon to the exiles of Israel as to those of Judah. So it would be, to expect from the religious principle which caused the return of the Jewish exiles, a still greater operative power on the exiles of Israel if it occasioned their return also. Moreover, it is not a groundless supposition to say that spiritually-minded individuals belonging to the Ten Tribes were present among the homeward wanderers of the year 536, etc. For if the persons mentioned in Ezra ii. 61 f. were not descendants[1] of citizens of that kingdom, yet there was, for example, Anna ἐκ φυλῆς 'Ασήρ at Jerusalem (Luke ii. 36; comp. Rev. vii. 4–8).

[1] Comp. Smend, Die Listen der Bücher Esra u. Nehemiah, p. 21, note.

Fifthly, nothing will be proved by such unfounded theories[1] as those which assert that the Israelitish religion, in passing through those stages which have furnished a subject for our contemplation, resembled other ancient religions, so that it might also have possibly shared the fate of those heathen creeds. To that we reply that no one is justified in assuming the possibility of the annihilation of the Old Testament religion, for facts give the lie to such a supposition. Since that faith has triumphantly survived all the external fortunes of its adherents, and was the marrow of the Israelitish nation, we must rather conclude that its extraordinary effects arose from extraordinary powers.

There are some, indeed, who do not admit that syllogism, and who "find it incomprehensible that any one should feel the necessity of representing the commencement of Israelitish history to himself in such a way that its later development should follow as a natural consequence."[2] Yet the scholar to whom we allude robs his objection of its force, because "he[3] expects to find in Israel's beginnings

---

[1] Smend, Die Genesis des Judenthums, p. 117.
[2] Smend in the passage last quoted.
[3] Ibid.; comp. also p. 95 of his work.

this and that peculiarity, which might point to the unexampled issue of its history." How much remains then of his objection? Only this, that "one must not set out with any preconceived idea whatever of Israel's commencement." Well, that may be easily promised him, and will be really followed out by those investigators of religious history who judge, as we do, of the motive-power of the Israelitish religion by the positive living proofs it has given. Moreover, he who warns others to beware of prejudices must himself avoid *à priori* theories; yet one of the first sentences with which Die Genesis des Judenthums begins contains either the prejudice that cause must not be judged by effect, or is directed against those weak logicians who, in coming to their conclusion on the cause by means of the effect, endeavour to carry back from the end of Old Testament religion into all its periods, and even to its beginning, not only the vital central ideas, but also their peripheric extensions — not only the pithy heart of the tree, but also all its leaves.

We, for our part, whilst judging of the beginning of Israelitish religion by its issue, only maintain that the immorality of Old Testament religion, surviving even the decay of the Ten Tribes, guarantees its independence of the natural power of Israel, as well as its own specific[1] difference from all ancient creeds, and we will do our utmost to prevent the profanation of holy Israel[2] from becoming the order of the day in Old Testament criticism.

[1] So that Tiele is wrong when he says (Geschiedenis, 1872, p. 526) : "The religion of Israel did not differ, even in its highest point of view, in kind or character from the worship of the surrounding and related nations." Comp. further, p. 527 f. Must not that writer confess (Compendium, 1880, p. 110 f.) that "gloomy misanthropy combined with voluptuous sensuality was a characteristic of all Semitic religions, Mosaic prophetism alone forming a favourable exception"?

[2] Compare, for example, Smend, Ueber den Genesis des Judenthums, p. 127 f. : "It is a unique fact that the small god of Jerusalem so powerfully raised his head when the Assyrians and Chaldæans apparently annhilated him."

CONCLUSION.

We now consider the assertion sufficiently proved that the fundamental elements of Old Testament religion were not altered by the writing prophets, and that the historical phases of the Mosaic religion were no change of its substance; and in the criticism of Old Testament history we regard that theory as correct which is defended by those expounders of natural life who stand aloof from evolutionist views of nature. The essential characteristic of the Israelitish religion, then, is connected with its origin, and only those things were secondary which did not affect its vital substance. It is as with a plant; even the germ shows the species which remains the same from first to last in the development of the plant, however great the variations of secondary marks, such as dimension, freshness, colouring, or fragrance may be.[1]

---

[1] This is an essential truth which suits Von der Alm's statement (ibid. p. 587), that "the Hebrews had also to pass through a course of development in their religious views."

The limitation which we have advocated of the field of Old Testament criticism has also been lately approved[1] by not a few investigators of religious knowledge. Even the long practised and far-seeing eye of Leopold Ranke was arrested by this conception of the religious history of Israel, as he was considering how he should weave the threads of Israel's history into the web of the development of mankind.[2]

[1] Comp. especially De Wette in Theologischen Studien und Kritiken (1837), pp. 983-987; Ernest Meier in the same periodical (1843), pp. 1021-1025; Diestel, Der Monotheismus des ältesten Heidenthums, vorzüglich bei den Semiten (Jahrbücher für Deutsche Theologie, 1860), particularly pp. 749, 759 f.; Dillmann, Ursprung der alttestamentlichen Religion (1865), p. 4 ff.; Schlottman in his article "Götzendienst," in Riehm's Handwörterbuch des Biblischen Alterthums; Victor von Strauss and Torney, Das unbewusst Weissagende im vorchristlichen Heidenthum (Zeitfragen des christl. Volkslebens, Heft 49, 1882), p. 36; Abr. Geiger, Das Judenthum und seine Geschichte, 2nd ed. (1865), pp. 20-22; Gratz, Geschichte der Israeliten, vol. i. (1874), pp. 15-22. Delff follows in the same track in his Grundzuge der Religionsgeschichte (1883), pp. 226 f., 256 f.

[2] Ranke, Weltgeschichte, vol. i. (1881) p. 30 ff.; see p. 32: "The idea of Jehovah did not arise from nature-worship; it is opposed to it;" p. 38: "In the simple course (progress) of a national nature-worship, there would have been no history of the human race. That first takes its rise in monotheism, which stands in direct opposition to nature-worship."

T. and T. Clark's Publications.

BY THE REV. JAMES STALKER, M.A.

Just published, in crown 8vo, price 3s. 6d., a New Edition, in larger Type, and handsomely bound,

THE LIFE OF JESUS CHRIST.

'No work since "Ecce Homo" has at all approached this in succinct, clear-cut, and incisive criticism on Christ as He appeared to those who believed on Him.'—*Literary World.*

'We are glad to welcome a new edition of this now celebrated work. . . . We trust, and confidently predict, that equal success will attend it in its new shape. . . . Mr. Stalker has produced a book without which no private library is complete.'—*Methodist Recorder.*

'Even with all our modern works on the exhaustless theme, from Neander to Farrar and Geikie, there is none which occupies the ground of Mr. Stalker's. . . . We question whether any one popular work so impressively and adequately represents Jesus to the mind. . . . It may be despised because it is small, but its light must shine.'—*Christian.*

Uniform with the above in size and price,

THE LIFE OF ST. PAUL.

'Even to those who know by heart the details of the great Apostle's life, this glowing sketch will be a revelation. Written with a fine sympathy for the more tender and personal aspects of his theme, Mr. Stalker has portrayed the outer and the inner life of Paul with a mingled power and beauty which is as rare as it is needed in evangelical writing.'—*Christian.*

'It is no matter of surprise that a new edition has so soon been called for. . . . It is a work of singular freshness.'—*Churchman.*

'A gem of sacred biography, which we have already commended to our readers. . . . Well does it deserve the new and handsome dress in which it now appears.'—*Christian Leader.*

Just published, in crown 8vo, price 3s. 6d.,

SCENES FROM THE LIFE OF JESUS.
Lectures
By Pastor E. LEHMANN.

'No one can read these lectures without gathering from them many holy and devotional thoughts.'—*Ecclesiastical Gazette.*

'We have seldom read lectures more deeply spiritual or more full of sober and thoughtful Scripture teaching.'—*Dublin Express.*

'There is in these lectures a tender sympathy, and a spiritual devoutness and simplicity, which gives to them a real charm.'—*Literary World.*

Just published, in demy 8vo, price 10s. 6d.,

THE KINGDOM OF GOD
BIBLICALLY AND HISTORICALLY CONSIDERED.
By JAS. S. CANDLISH, D.D.

'A charming book, written with unaffected, easy, and perfect lucidity, and therefore to be read with delight. Perhaps a magic pen belongs to the house of Candlish. . . . The book is positively good, and ought to be thoroughly popular with the larger religious public.'—*Monthly Interpreter.*

'As to the ability of this volume there can be no question; it is of profound interest.'—*Evangelical Magazine.*

✳

Just published, in crown 8vo, price 6s.,

OLD AND NEW THEOLOGY:
A CONSTRUCTIVE CRITIQUE.

By Rev. J. B. HEARD, M.A.

'We can promise all real students of Holy Scripture who have found their way out of some of the worst of the scholastic byelanes and ruts, and are striving to reach the broad and firm high road that leads to the Eternal City, a real treat from the perusal of these pages. Progressive theologians, who desire to find "the old in the new, and the new in the old," will be deeply grateful to Mr. Heard for this courageous and able work.'—*Christian World.*

'Among the many excellent theological works, whether English or German, published by Messrs. Clark, there are few that deserve more careful study than this book. ... It cannot fail to charm by its grace of style, and to supply food for solid thought.'—*Dublin Express.*

BY THE SAME AUTHOR.

Fifth Edition, in crown 8vo, price 6s.,

THE TRIPARTITE NATURE OF MAN:
SPIRIT, SOUL, AND BODY.

Applied to Illustrate and Explain the Doctrines of Original Sin, the New Birth, the Disembodied State, and the Spiritual Body.

'The author has got a striking and consistent theory. Whether agreeing or disagreeing with that theory, it is a book which any student of the Bible may read with pleasure.'—*Guardian.*

'An elaborate, ingenious, and very able book.'—*London Quarterly Review.*

Just published, in demy 8vo, price 9s.,

THE DOCTRINE OF THE HOLY SPIRIT.

(The Ninth Series of the Cunningham Lectures.)

By GEORGE SMEATON, D.D.,
Professor of Exegetical Theology, New College, Edinburgh.

'The theological student will be benefited by a careful perusal of this survey, and that not for the moment, but through all his future life.'—*Watchman.*

'Very cordially do we commend these able and timely lectures to the notice of our readers. Every theological student should master them.'—*Baptist Magazine.*

'It is a pleasure to meet with a work like this. ... Our brief account, we trust, will induce the desire to study this work.'—*Dickinson's Theological Quarterly.*

Just published, in Two Volumes, 8vo (1600 pages), price 28s.,

THE DOCTRINE OF SACRED SCRIPTURE:

A CRITICAL, HISTORICAL, AND DOGMATIC INQUIRY INTO THE ORIGIN AND NATURE OF THE OLD AND NEW TESTAMENTS.

By GEORGE T. LADD, D.D.,
PROFESSOR OF MENTAL AND MORAL PHILOSOPHY YALE COLLEGE.

'This important work is pre-eminently adapted for students, and treats in an exhaustive manner nearly every important subject of Biblical criticism which is agitating the religious mind at the present day.'—*Contemporary Review.*

Just published, in crown 8vo, price 6s.,

STUDIES IN THE CHRISTIAN EVIDENCES.
By ALEXANDER MAIR, D.D.

'This book ought to be immensely popular. . . . Speaking from our own experience of works of this character, we have no hesitation in saying that, for readers in general, we know of no work which is so distinctly suited for all who can understand a complete subject, made remarkably easy and clear. . . . That one chapter on the "Unique Personality of Christ" is a masterpiece of eloquent writing, though it is scarcely fair to mention one portion where every part is excellent. The beauties of the volume are everywhere apparent, and therefore will again attract the mind that has been once delighted with the literary feast.'—*Rock.*

'Dr. Mair has made an honest study of Strauss, Renan, Keim, and "Supernatural Religion," and his book is an excellent one to put into the hands of doubters and inquirers.'—*English Churchman.*

Just published, in crown 8vo, price 6s.,

CHRISTIAN CHARITY IN THE ANCIENT CHURCH.
By G. UHLHORN, D.D.

'The historical knowledge this work displays is immense, and the whole subject is wrought out with great care and skill; it is a most readable, delightful, and instructive volume.'—*Evangelical Christendom.*

Just published, in demy 8vo, price 10s. 6d.,

THE LORD'S PRAYER:
A Practical Meditation.
By REV. NEWMAN HALL, LL.B.

'Short, crisp sentences, absolute in form and lucid in thought, convey the author's meaning and carry on his exposition. . . . He is impatient of dim lights; his thoughts are sharply cut and are like crystals in their clearness.'—*British Quarterly Review.*

'Well deserves a place in the minister's library.'—*Literary World.*

In demy 8vo, price 9s.,

OUTLINES OF THE HISTORY OF CHRISTIAN DOCTRINE.

By Rev. T. G. CRIPPEN.

'The essence of a whole library is included in Mr. Crippen's "History of Christian Doctrine." . . . It is a scholarly work, and must have entailed an incalculable amount of research and discrimination.'—*Clergyman's Magazine.*

In crown 8vo, price 5s.,

MODERN PHYSICS.

HISTORICAL AND PHILOSOPHICAL STUDIES.

By ERNEST NAVILLE.

'Christian scientists should at once procure this learned and able volume.'—*Evangelical Magazine.*

'Full of learning, and marked by much original thought.'—*British Quarterly Review.*

In demy 8vo, price 9s.,

LECTURES ON PAUL'S EPISTLES TO THE THESSALONIANS.

By JOHN HUTCHISON, D.D.

'Certainly one of the ablest and best commentaries that we have ever read. The style is crisp and clear; and the scholarship is in no sense of a superficial or pretentious order.'—*Evangelical Magazine.*

Just published, in crown 8vo, price 2s. 6d.,

THE WORK OF THE HOLY SPIRIT IN MAN.

Discourses,

By Pastor G. TOPHEL,

GENEVA.

'An admirable book on a subject of the deepest importance. We do not remember any work on this theme that is more impressive, or seems more fitted for general usefulness.'—*British Messenger.*

In Three Volumes, 8vo, price 31s. 6d.,

THE LIFE OF CHRIST.
By Dr. BERNHARD WEISS,
PROFESSOR OF THEOLOGY, BERLIN.

'This book seems destined to hold a very distinguished, if not absolutely unique place in the criticism of the New Testament. Its fearless search after truth, its independence of spirit, its extent of research, its thoughtful and discriminating tone, must secure for it a very high reputation.'—*Congregationalist.*

BY THE SAME AUTHOR.

In Two Volumes, 8vo, price 21s.,

BIBLICAL THEOLOGY OF THE NEW TESTAMENT.

'The work which this volume completes is one of no ordinary strength and acumen. It is an exposition of the books of the New Testament arranged scientifically, that is, according to the authorship and development. It is the ripe fruit of many years of New Testament exegesis and theological study. . . . The book is in every way a notable one.'—*British Quarterly Review.*

In Four Volumes, 8vo, price £2, 2s.,

A SYSTEM OF CHRISTIAN DOCTRINE.
By Dr. I. A. DORNER,
PROFESSOR OF THEOLOGY, BERLIN.

'The work has many and great excellences, and is really indispensable to all who would obtain a thorough acquaintance with the great problems of theology. It is a great benefit to English students that it should be made accessible to them in their own language, and in a form so elegant and convenient.'—*Literary Churchman.*

In Three Volumes, 8vo, price 31s. 6d.,

CHRISTIAN ETHICS.
By Dr. H. MARTENSEN,
BISHOP OF SEELAND.

𝔗𝔯𝔞𝔫𝔰𝔩𝔞𝔱𝔢𝔡 𝔣𝔯𝔬𝔪 𝔱𝔥𝔢 𝔄𝔲𝔱𝔥𝔬𝔯'𝔰 𝔊𝔢𝔯𝔪𝔞𝔫 𝔈𝔡𝔦𝔱𝔦𝔬𝔫.

VOLUME I.—GENERAL ETHICS.
  „   II.—INDIVIDUAL ETHICS.
  „   III.—SOCIAL ETHICS.

'It is no ordinary book, and we commend it to the study of all who are interested in Christian Ethics, as one of the most able treatises on the subject which has ever yet appeared.'—*Watchman.*

'Dr. Martensen's work on Christian Dogmatics reveals the strength of thought as well as the fine literary grace of its author. . . . His chief ethical writings comprise a system of Christian Ethics, general and special, in three volumes. Each of these volumes has great and singular excellence, and it might be generally felt that in them the author has surpassed his own work on "Christian Dogmatics."'—Rev. Principal CAIRNS.

T. and T. Clark's Publications.

HERZOG'S ENCYCLOPÆDIA.

Now Complete, in Three Volumes, imperial 8vo, price 24s. each,

ENCYCLOPÆDIA

OR

DICTIONARY

OF

BIBLICAL, HISTORICAL, DOCTRINAL, AND PRACTICAL THEOLOGY.

Based on the Real-Encyklopädie of Herzog, Plitt, and Hauck.

EDITED BY

Professor PHILIP SCHAFF, D.D., LL.D.,

UNION THEOLOGICAL SEMINARY, NEW YORK.

'It is certain that this Encyclopædia will fill a place in our theological literature, in which, for a long time, it will have no rival.'—Prof. HODGE, *Princeton*.

'This Encyclopædia is exceedingly well done. . . . We hope that this new enterprise will be successful, and that no minister's library will long remain without a copy of this work. . . To people in the country, far from libraries, who cannot lay their hands on books, a work of this kind would simply be invaluable.'—*Daily Review.*

'We have been delighted with its comprehensiveness. We have never failed to find what we wanted.'—*Edinburgh Courant.*

'As a comprehensive work of reference, within a moderate compass, we know nothing at all equal to it in the large department which it deals with.'—*Church Bells.*

'The work will remain as a wonderful monument of industry, learning, and skill. It will be indispensable to the student of specifically Protestant theology; nor, indeed, do we think that any scholar, whatever be his especial line of thought or study, would find it superfluous on his shelves.'—*Literary Churchman.*

'We commend this work with a touch of enthusiasm, for we have often wanted such ourselves. It embraces in its range of writers all the leading authors of Europe on ecclesiastical questions. A student may deny himself many other volumes to secure this, for it is certain to take a prominent and permanent place in our literature.'—*Evangelical Magazine.*

T. and T. Clark's Publications.

In One Volume, 8vo, Second Edition, price 12s.,
FINAL CAUSES.
By PAUL JANET, Member of the Institute, Paris.
TRANSLATED FROM THE FRENCH BY WILLIAM AFFLECK, B.D.

'This very learned, accurate, and, within its prescribed limits, exhaustive work. . . . The book as a whole abounds in matter of the highest interest, and is a model of learning and judicious treatment.'—*Guardian.*

'Illustrated and defended with an ability and learning which must command the reader's admiration.'—*Dublin Review.*

'A great contribution to the literature of this subject. M. Janet has mastered the conditions of the problem, is at home in the literature of science and philosophy; . . . in clearness, vigour, and depth it has been seldom equalled, and more seldom excelled, in philosophical literature.'—*Spectator.*

'A wealth of scientific knowledge and a logical acumen which will win the admiration of every reader.'—*Church Quarterly Review.*

BY THE SAME AUTHOR.
Just published, in demy 8vo, price 10s. 6d.,
THE THEORY OF MORALS.
TRANSLATED FROM THE LATEST FRENCH EDITION.

'As remarkable for the force and beauty of its form of expression as for its vast and varied learning, its philosophical acumen, and its uniform attitude of reverence toward religious and moral problems of the most transcendent interest to mankind.'—*Literary World.*

'This book is really a valuable addition to the literature of the subject. . . . Let the student of morals and religion read it for himself. It is pleasant reading, and the translation seems to us in every respect admirable.'—*Watchman.*

Just published, in demy 8vo, price 10s. 6d.,
THE PARABLES OF JESUS.
A METHODICAL EXPOSITION.
By SIEGFRIED GOEBEL, Court Chaplain in Halberstadt.
TRANSLATED BY PROF. J. S. BANKS, HEADINGLEY COLLEGE.

'This ought to be one of the most helpful of all the volumes in the "Foreign Theological Library." . . . Such expositions as those of the Good Samaritan and the Prodigal Son are as full of human feeling as others are of ripe learning. The volume is quite a treasury of original exposition on a subject on which preachers constantly need help, and on which little that is new has appeared in recent years.'—*Methodist Recorder.*

In crown 8vo, price 4s. 6d.,
THE WORLD OF PRAYER;
Or, Prayer in Relation to Personal Religion.
By BISHOP MONRAD.

'One of the richest devotional books that we have read.'—*Primitive Methodist Magazine.*

T. and T. Clark's Publications.

In demy 8vo, Third Edition, price 10s. 6d.,

THE TRAINING OF THE TWELVE;
OR,
EXPOSITION OF PASSAGES IN THE GOSPELS EXHIBITING THE TWELVE DISCIPLES OF JESUS UNDER DISCIPLINE FOR THE APOSTLESHIP.

By A. B. BRUCE, D.D.,
PROFESSOR OF DIVINITY, FREE CHURCH COLLEGE, GLASGOW.

'Here we have a really great book on an important, large, and attractive subject—a book full of loving, wholesome, profound thoughts about the fundamentals of Christian faith and practice.'—*British and Foreign Evangelical Review.*

'It is some five or six years since this work first made its appearance, and now that a second edition has been called for, the author has taken the opportunity to make some alterations which are likely to render it still more acceptable. Substantially, however, the book remains the same, and the hearty commendation with which we noted its first issue applies to it at least as much now.'—*Rock.*

BY THE SAME AUTHOR.

In demy 8vo, Second Edition, price 10s. 6d.,

THE HUMILIATION OF CHRIST,
IN ITS PHYSICAL, ETHICAL, AND OFFICIAL ASPECTS.
SIXTH SERIES OF CUNNINGHAM LECTURES.

'These lectures are able and deep-reaching to a degree not often found in the religious literature of the day; withal, they are fresh and suggestive. . . . The learning and the deep and sweet spirituality of this discussion will commend it to many faithful students of the truth as it is in Jesus.'—*Congregationalist.*

'We have not for a long time met with a work so fresh and suggestive as this of Professor Bruce. . . . We do not know where to look at our English Universities for a treatise so calm, logical, and scholarly.'—*English Independent.*

KEIL AND DELITZSCH'S
INTRODUCTION TO AND COMMENTARIES ON THE OLD TESTAMENT.
In 27 Volumes, demy 8vo.

MESSRS. CLARK have resolved to offer complete sets of this work at the Original Subscription Price of £7, 2s. Single volumes may be had, price 10s. 6d.

'This series is one of great importance to the Biblical scholar; and as regards its general execution, it leaves little or nothing to be desired.'—*Edinburgh Review.*

www.ingramcontent.com/pod-product-compliance
Lightning Source LLC
Chambersburg PA
CBHW021730220426
43662CB00008B/778